T0366208

MADE TO SERVE

MADE TO SERVE

How manufacturers can
compete through servitization and
product–service systems

TIM BAINES AND HOWARD LIGHTFOOT

WILEY

Registered office

John Wiley & Sons Ltd, The Atrium, Southern Gate, Chichester, West Sussex, PO19 8SQ, United Kingdom

For details of our global editorial offices, for customer services and for information about how to apply for permission to reuse the copyright material in this book please see our website at www.wiley.com.

Wiley publishes in a variety of print and electronic formats and by print-on-demand. Some material included with standard print versions of this book may not be included in e-books or in print-on-demand. If this book refers to media such as a CD or DVD that is not included in the version you purchased, you may download this material at http://booksupport.wiley.com. For more information about Wiley products, visit www.wiley.com.

Designations used by companies to distinguish their products are often claimed as trademarks. All brand names and product names used in this book are trade names, service marks, trademarks or registered trademarks of their respective owners. The publisher is not associated with any product or vendor mentioned in this book.

Library of Congress Cataloging-in-Publication Data

Baines, Tim, 1962–

    Made to serve : how manufacturers can compete through servitization and product–service systems / Tim Baines and Howard Lightfoot.

        pages cm

    Includes index.

    ISBN 978-1-118-58531-3 (cloth) – ISBN 978-1-118-58527-6 (ebk) – ISBN 978-1-118-58528-3 (ebk) – ISBN 978-1-118-58529-0 (ebk)   1. Manufacturing industries.   2. Warranty.   I. Lightfoot, Howard, 1947–   II. Title.

    HD9720.5.B35 2013

    658.8'12–dc23

                                         2012049218

A catalogue record for this book is available from the British Library.

ISBN 978-1-118-58531-3 (hardback)   ISBN 978-1-118-58527-6 (ebk)
ISBN 978-1-118-58528-3 (ebk)   ISBN 978-1-118-58529-0 (ebk)

Cover design: Rogue Four Design

Set in 12/16 pt Dante Mt Std by Toppan Best-set Premedia Limited, Hong Kong
Printed in Great Britain by TJ International Ltd, Padstow, Cornwall, UK

To Captain . . . thank you (TB)
To my son Gavin, who always fills me with pride (HL)

CONTENTS

PREFACE

Manufacturing and services industries are often seen as independent. Whether discussing the economies of nations, classification of businesses, education and training, or employment, they are treated as separate. Yet manufacturers themselves can base their competitive strategies on services, and the process through which this is achieved is commonly known as servitization (or servicization). The commercial benefits of servitization are convincing (Rolls-Royce Plc earn around 50% of their revenue from services); the environmental arguments compelling (significant reductions in materials and energy usage); and the opportunities immense (three-quarters of wealth worldwide is now created through services).

Servitization can be approached in various ways. Some manufacturers simply add more and more individual services to complement their product offerings, while others develop bespoke, long-term and intimate offerings with a few strategic customers. Seeing themselves as service providers, they exploit their own design and production competences to deliver and improve business processes for their customers. We refer to this latter category as advanced services. These product–service systems demand dramatically different operations to those of production, but when done well are highly valuable to the commercial and environmental sustainability of the manufacturer. The challenge is to understand these services, what they can look like in practice, how to deliver them successfully, and when it makes sense to do so. Our purpose is to guide conventional manufacturers through this challenge.

The book is laid out in four parts. First, we explain why services-based competitive strategies are increasingly appealing by reflecting on the wider business context that is now common for manufacturers. Second, we examine different forms of services, their financial benefits and the risks they incur, and introduce an organizational system for their successful delivery. Third, we describe the practices and technologies that constitute this system. We explain and illustrate each in detail, examining their role and significance in the delivery of advanced services. In the final part of this book we help managers to evaluate the relevance of servitization to their own manufacturing organization.

This book is intended to impact on industrial practice. Our goal is to guide the thoughts and actions of senior executives, managers and engineers, within manufacturing business, that are debating the value and consequences of a servitization strategy. In this way, it is also intended to support students on vocational educational programmes. Servitization is treated from the viewpoint of the conventional manufacturer. The content draws heavily on the practices of leading companies such as Rolls-Royce, MAN Truck and Bus, Caterpillar (and dealers), Alstom and Xerox, together with relevant research in this field. Over recent years we have extensively studied the journeys of these companies to become successfully servitized manufacturers. As for style, we have set out to be pragmatic and use a straightforward language that is frequently illustrated with data and examples, with each section beginning with a quick reference guide.

So, is the scope of this book relevant to your organization? Don't be put off by the strange word of servitization; all manufacturers can gain some value through services if they are delivered efficiently and effectively. Similarly while we expect manufacturers who operate in a business-to-business environment to readily associate with our book, the terminology and examples we use simply reflect and celebrate that much progress has been made by such companies to compete through services. If your organization has engineering and production competences, then this book is relevant. Indeed, as we point out later, these competences are foundational to success through servitization.

FOREWORD

Manufactured goods, whether they be high cost capital machinery or vehicles, are becoming more and more commoditized. Globalization and use of technology has enabled such items to be produced at much lower costs and there has also been a significant increase in the speed of imitation and copying.

It is no longer sufficient to justify the capital cost of such goods with the standard explanation of the features and benefits. Such claims are increasingly required by the customer to be underwritten with lifetime service agreements and guaranteed cost of operation.

This is the essence of the transformation to a servitized organization that manufacturers need to consider if they are to sustain future business and differentiate themselves from the competition.

In my experience this is a transformation that is not easy and may not be for every organization. It is not only technology that is forcing these changes but increasingly cultural, leadership and management capabilities that are being tested.

The real challenge for a servitized organization is that you put yourself in the shoes of the customer and experience what it is like to deal with your own organization. The benefits of such a transformation is that you become part of feedback loop that enables the organization to evaluate the performance of the product 'in service' and if executed correctly will ring fence the business from the competition whilst providing valuable R&D information for future product development.

In the case of MAN Truck and Bus the product is the entry ticket into a future business/profit stream that is obtained from the financing, servicing and parts supply through the life of the vehicle. It also proves the point that in the capital goods market that sales sell the first item but all future sales depend on your service organization. This is where reputations, brand image, customer satisfaction and retention as well as profitability are determined.

In this book Tim and Howard describe how organizations are configured when they are successful at servitization, and how this differs to the more conventional view of manufacturing. Quite simply they present a pragmatic vision of a future for many manufacturers in developed economies.

Des Evans, CEO, MAN Truck and Bus UK Ltd

Chapter 1

The world once seemed simple, manufacturers made things and services companies did things for us. Today, more and more manufacturers are competing through a portfolio of integrated products and services. This is a services-led competitive strategy, and the process through which it is achieved is commonly referred to as servitization. Celebrated icons of such strategies in action include Rolls-Royce, Xerox and Alstom, who all offer some form of extended maintenance, repair and overhaul contracts where revenue generation is directly linked to asset availability, reliability and performance.

Servitization is, however, much more than simply adding services to existing products within a few large multinational companies. It's potentially about viewing the manufacturer as a service provider. A service provider that sets out to improve the processes of their customers through a business model rather than product-based innovation. The manufacturer then exploits its design and production-based competences to give widespread improvements in efficiency and effectiveness to the customer.

Manufacturers have, however, traditionally focused their efforts on product innovation and cost reduction. Companies such as Porsche and Ferrari have been celebrated for bringing new and exciting designs into the market, while companies such as Toyota have been held in awe for their work with Lean production systems. These successes can foster a perception that the only way for manufacturing to underpin competitiveness is through new materials and technologies, faster and more reliable automation, machining with more precision, waste reduction programmes, smoother flow of parts, employee engagement, and closer coupling within the supply chain.

Services offer a third way to compete. This is not an 'instead of' or 'easy option' for companies that are struggling to succeed. Indeed, delivering some types of advanced services can require a set of technologies and practices that are every bit as demanding as those in production. Neither does this require the manufacturer to abandon its technology strengths; instead these can be developed to help ensure long term competitiveness. Consequently, there is a growing realization that such services hold high-value potential.

Ironically, manufacturers competing on the basis of service provision is not a new phenomenon. In the 1800s, International Harvester used services to help establish their new reaping equipment among farmers in the American Midwest. Similarly, origins of power-by-the-hour lie partially in the practices of Bristol Siddeley in the 1960s. Perhaps what is new is our willingness as a business community to recognize that 'manufacturing' is not just about product innovation, process technologies and production. We are abandoning a production-centric paradigm to embrace a broader view of manufacturing.

A few manufacturers have been following this route for some time. To illustrate, over the past 20 years there has been an intense debate in the West about the rights and wrongs of outsourcing and off-shoring to China and India. Many in manufacturing have held out hope that the tide would in some way turn. While some production activities have been relinquished, key manufacturers have been quietly moving forward in their supply chains to take over service activities carried out by their customers. Services have been key to their survival, and as a consequence our language and perceptions are now changing.

Conventional manufacturers can struggle, however, to appreciate the value of services. Managers often seek such a simple explanation of servitization that they fail to appreciate how such a strategy is likely to be of significant benefit. This is often the case with organizational rather than technological innovations. In the early 1980s it was difficult to imagine that 'Just-in-Time' would endure, and yet today it's hard to identify a single manufacturing company that has not been touched by Lean techniques in one way or another.

Servitization is a similar paradigm shift. Success requires managers to hold a different mindset or worldview to their colleagues in production. The challenge is equivalent to persuading a manager skilled in Lean techniques to appreciate the value in craft production. Yet some niche producers excel through their exploitation of such systems (e.g. Holland & Holland in their manufacture of high-value sporting guns). *So, how can the value of services be thoroughly introduced and explained to those who are more familiar with a production-centric view of the world?* This is the challenge we have taken up in this book.

Our purpose is to guide conventional manufacturers through the concept of servitization. To achieve this we have tackled the topic in four progressive steps. First, we set about illustrating the conditions in the business world that are causing services to become increasingly relevant for manufacturers. Second, we give illustrations and examples of a services-led competitive strategy, and pay particular attention to those 'advanced' services that are widely associated with servitization. Third, we paint a picture of what it takes to compete on the basis of advanced services, and delve into the technologies and practices that leading manufacturers have adopted. Finally, we summarize the conditions that favour the take-up of servitization within a manufacturer.

Collectively, these four parts outline a potential organizational transformation. Our goal has been to explain servitization in such a way that mainstream manufactures will, through following this book, be better equipped to fully understand the relevance of this concept to their broader operations.

1.1 Terminology and Scope

The word 'services' conjures up a variety of interpretations. The later sections of this book will clarify many of the key terms in detail. Here we give a few critical descriptions that provide a foundation for the following chapter and indicate the general scope of the book – as the following headings indicate.

This book deals with manufacturers

All forms of organizations deliver services. In everyday life we come across many organizations that seem entirely engaged with delivering services alone, such as banks, insurance brokers, local government, schools, and hospitals. Sometimes these companies use product nomenclature (for example, an insurance product or a mortgage product) and have many similarities with conventional production systems. However, we consider these as 'pure-service providers' and do not study them further.

This book is written for those businesses that engage in product manufacture. We adopt a broad definition of manufacturing and take it to mean that the company has some authority over the design and production of the products with which it deals. We recognize that this terminology does not rest comfortably with some companies who are advanced in servitization. Xerox, for instance, would describe themselves as a services-led technology company; others might choose to be known as a solutions business or services provider. However, we use the term manufacturing simply to anchor the content of this book, and draw a distinction for these organizations from pure-service providers.

Our intention is to impact all forms of manufacturing. Unfortunately many of the leading examples of servitization are businesses which are large, and produce expensive and technically complex products. Yet such companies are not our exclusive target; many lessons in this book are generally applicable.

Manufacturers servitizing through advanced services

The word service can be used in different ways. For example, service can refer to how well an action is performed ('that was good service'). Alternatively it can be used to refer to an activity; (e.g., helpdesk, maintenance, training or spare parts provision). Our focus is on the latter use of the word service; activities that a manufacturer can perform to complement the products it produces. All manufacturers offer services to some extent, but some establish market differentiation through these, and so can be thought of as following services-led competitive strategies.

Servitization is a term given to a transformation. It is about manufacturers increasingly offering services integrated with their products. Of these, some manufacturers choose to servitize by offering an extensive portfolio of relatively conventional services. Others move almost entirely into pure services, largely independent of their products, and provide offerings such as general consulting. Others still move to deliver advanced services.

Advanced services are a special case in servitization. Sometimes known as outcome, capability or availability contracts, here the manufacturer delivers services (coupled with incentivized contracting mechanisms) that are critical to their customers' core business processes. The contracts associated with this type of offering frequently

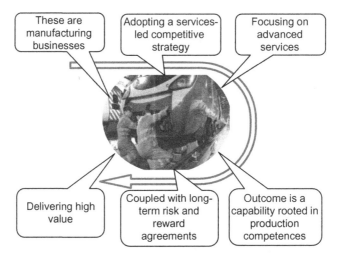

Figure 1.1: *The servitization route addressed in this book*

extend over many years, with the manufacturer adopting greater risk by taking responsibility for the performance of its products, and being rewarded through ongoing and more profitable revenue streams. 'Power-by-the-hour', as offered by Rolls-Royce, is an iconic example of such a service.

These advanced services can hold high value for manufacturers. They can help strengthen relationships, lock out competitors, grow revenues and profits. As a consequence these are the services on which this book is concerned. Our particular focus is on manufacturers taking bold moves into providing advanced services as summarized in Figure 1.1.

Advanced services are delivered through product–service systems (PSS)

Servitization involves both the innovation of the service offering and also the innovation of the manufacturer's internal capabilities in operations. This delivery system is just as important as the offering itself. Just as Henry Ford changed the world, not just through the design of his automobile (the Model T), but also his system of mass production that enabled high volumes of products to be produced at a very low price.

Production systems deliver products; advanced services are delivered by product–service systems. These systems are based on very different interactions with the customer. Figure 1.2 illustrates how each of these systems may appear, based around the example of the provision of excavator equipment.

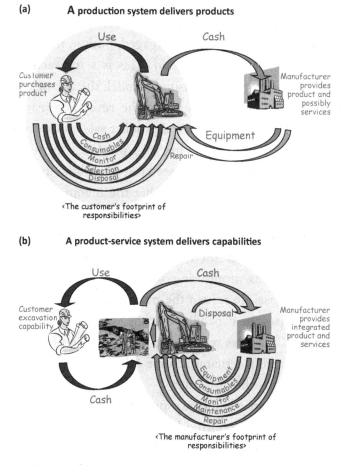

Figure 1.2: *Contrasts between a production system and product–service system*

In the production world the manufacturer produces the equipment (the excavator in Figure 1.2). When this is sold the manufacturer is rewarded financially. Although the customer may only want to use the equipment, to do so it has to first raise finance for its purchase, and then provide the necessary consumables (e.g. fuel, lubrication, tyres). They also have to monitor the equipment's performance and, should a problem begin to arise, the customer invariably performs some diagnostics before then arranging maintenance and repair. These services may well be carried out by either the customer themselves, the original manufacturer, or an independent repair shop on the customer's behalf. Eventually the equipment wears and needs replacing. Once again the customer becomes engaged, both in new equipment selection, and the disposal of the old. This is a transactional-based 'production and consumption' business model; the responsibilities of ownership lie with the customer, and the revenue stream for the manufacturer is largely based around product sale and spare parts.

Within a PSS, the manufacturer still produces the equipment. However, ownership and the associated responsibilities are not necessarily transferred to the customer; rather the manufacturer sets out to provide a 'capability' (an excavation capability in the case of Figure 1.2). Understanding the customer's requirement, the manufacturer rather than the customer then takes responsibility for equipment selection, consumables, monitoring of performance, and carrying out servicing and disposal. In return the manufacturer receives payment as the customer uses the capability that the equipment provides. This is a 'value in use' business model; the responsibilities for equipment performance lie with the manufacturer, who receives revenue as the equipment is used by the customer.

Neither production systems nor product–service systems operate in isolation. Both are supported by an ecosystem of suppliers and partners; but the roles of these differ from one system to another. In particular, the financial partner is a critical enabler that is often overlooked. *Try asking how a manufacturer such as Rolls-Royce affords to provide gas turbines typically costing $10,000,000 on a power-by-the-hour contract? How can they afford to 'own' the gas turbine on their balance sheet?* In this instance partners such as International Leasing and Financing Company (ILFC) can finance the purchase of the turbine and then lease it to the customer (user). This fee then forms part of the customer's monthly payments on the power-by-the-hour contract. We will explore the role of suppliers later in the book, and pay particular attention to how they enable this financial model.

Product-service systems significantly impact the operations of the manufacturer

This book focuses on the broad operations of the servitized manufacturer. Just as many authors have given their attention to understanding Lean practices and technologies that support production, our goal has been to understand the system that has to be created to deliver advanced services efficiently and effectively.

The practices and technologies differ in six key areas. As summarized in Figure 1.3, those manufacturers who are successful in the

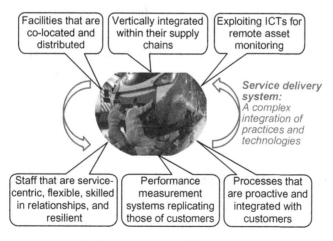

Figure 1.3: *Practices and technologies key to delivering advanced services*

delivery of advanced services create facilities that are co-located and distributed throughout customers' operations; these are vertically integrated to ensure control over responsiveness and continuous improvement, and are staffed by personnel who are flexible, relationship builders, service-centric, authentic, technically adept and resilient. These people work with processes that are integrated into their customer's operations and, supported by remote asset monitoring, help to manage proactively the condition, use and location of assets in the field. The whole system is controlled by measures that are those of the customer and focused on outcomes, and yet complemented by tactics that broadly demonstrate value across the operations.

Occasionally this is described as a 'service delivery system' for advanced services. Such terminology is sometimes favoured by scholars as it helps to capture the complexities, interactions and interdependencies of delivering these services. We use such terms sparingly, and instead favour more traditional terminology that is more readily understood by practitioners. We must though emphasize that we take a broad view of operations, and include within our scope the interactions with customers and partners that come together in a broad relationship to deliver services.

A final note on scope. The challenges of servitization reach beyond operations. Success demands the right offering, to the right customer, for the right application. In this way, the content we present is intended as a complement to texts that, for example, examine the design and marketing of services.

1.2 Knowledge Base

This book represents the culmination of an extensive research programme that has set out to understand in-depth the strategies of

world-leading servitized manufacturers. When we started on this programme we realized that our success would depend critically on:

1. *Industrial excellence with relevance:* We had to engage with manufacturers who were both demonstrating outstanding success in
   delivering what we would later recognize as advanced services,
   and would generally be seen as mainstream producers. We would
   need to avoid somewhat specialist manufacturers who, though
   they might be successful, would be difficult for the broader community to identify with.

2. *Breadth with depth:* We had to examine the entire system of practices and technologies that enable manufacturers to deliver on
   servitization. To succeed we would need to engage personnel
   ranging from senior executives dealing with an organization's
   strategy through to field technicians delivering on-site services.
   And we would need to do this across a range of organizations.

3. *Rigour with translation:* We had to execute our work following the
   conventions and rigours of scientific research. Only by following
   such a process could we be confident in our findings and also their
   limitations. However, we also needed to recognize that rarely do
   practitioners have the time or inclination to wade through scientific papers. We would need to explain our findings succinctly in a
   straightforward style.

Our knowledge base was therefore derived from three sources.
First, throughout this programme we have studied closely Rolls-
Royce Civil Aerospace, Alstom Transport (particularly the Train Life
Services division), Caterpillar (including selected dealers in the UK and
USA), MAN Truck and Bus and Xerox. Table 1.1 gives a brief introduction to the principal activities of these core collaborators. These companies have been exceptional hosts. In all cases they have granted
access to their facilities, introduced our team to partners within their
extended supply chain, and arranged interviews with key customers.

Table 1.1 Examples of advanced services

	Rolls-Royce	Alstom Transport	MAN	Caterpillar and dealers	Xerox
Generic name	TotalCare	Train Life Services	Fleet Management	Equipment Management Services	Managed Print Services
Customers include	Cathay Pacific, United Airlines, Singapore Airlines	Virgin Trains Tubelines Arriva Trains Wales First Group	Wincanton Distribution, Hoyer Logistics	Rio Tinto AngloGold Ashanti	Newport City Council Fiat Group Proctor and Gamble
Service activities include	Predictive maintenance, logistics management, global repair and overhaul	Maintenance, renovation, spare parts management and technical support	Inspection, maintenance and worthiness, along with visibility of driver and vehicle performance	Monitoring condition, use and location, preventive maintenance, unscheduled repair	Multi-brand print, fleet management, document management, print infrastructure optimization
Delivered by	Rolls-Royce, and as joint ventures	Alstom	MAN/independent distributors	Caterpillar dealerships	OEM and partner resellers/distributors
Typical duration	Ten years	Twenty–thirty years	Five years	Two–ten years	One–five years
Basis of revenue received/penalized	Fixed dollar per flying hour/hours out of service	Miles travelled/lost passenger hours Lost customer hours	Miles travelled/time out of service	Fixed dollar per operating hour/hours out of service	Pay per copy, reduced 'total cost of ownership'

Typical characteristics

To illustrate, at Caterpillar we conducted multiple case studies of their own operations as well as key dealers and customers in Europe and the USA. Such studies included facility visits, in-depth interviews with staff ranging from vice presidents through to field service engineers and operatives, and the collection of a broad data set about performance and practices.

We are extremely grateful for the openness shown by our core collaborators. In return, we have taken care to protect the anonymity of individual personnel and avoid reference to overly specific company data. It is important to stress that although our case companies have engaged with us throughout the research process, the interpretations presented across these companies are our own.

Second, this in-depth process has been complemented by also looking across a wide range of industries. While our core collaborations have allowed us to dig deep into services and their delivery, we have also surveyed many other manufacturing companies to ensure that we have a broad and representative knowledge base. Execution of the programme soon revealed that we would not be able to share the names of organizations and people with which we have worked. Many businesses were, for example, willing to grant access and share their experiences only on the condition that we would not reveal their identity when presenting and discussing our results. We have respected their requests.

Finally, we have systematically reviewed articles, reports and papers emanating from the wider research base. As part of this process we have held hundreds of conversations and private briefings with managers and engineers, along with workshops, conferences and industry forums. We have ourselves contributed to conferences and journals, and received feedback from the respective research communities on our contributions.

Our resultant knowledge base is a distillation of the data from these three sources. Yet there have also been many people who have contributed, both directly and indirectly, to this programme of research. Many academic and industrial colleagues have provided critiques of our work and suggestions on how to improve. We are immensely grateful for their input. In Appendix 1 we acknowledge their participation in, and contribution to, this study.

1.3 What's New Here?

Our purpose is to guide manufacturers through the concept of servitization, in particular advanced services, and how to deliver these successfully. *So, what is new about this topic, and what is new in this book?*

Our challenge with this topic has been twofold. Those readers who are new to servitization will want to feel enlightened and enthused, while those who are familiar with the topic will demand to know significantly more about its complex concepts. This challenge is formidable in itself, but heightened by the limitations in the current knowledge base on servitization. There are particular tensions with:

1. *Exemplars:* Most of the examples are from large multinational companies delivering expensive and complex equipment to a relatively small set of customers, whereas many manufacturers are producing high volumes of products for a large range of customers.
2. *Research:* Most research focuses on these business-to-business applications because these are the companies claiming success through services. Many researchers want to broaden their scope, but are faced with a critical question. *Who is successful with servitization?* It's quite natural to want to refer to financial records of performance, but rarely do these provide sufficient insight into the performance of a services business within a manufacturer.
3. *Expectations:* Servitization is seen as a new concept that is not commonly understood; expectations are high. A simple explanation of the topic rarely leaves the practitioner confident that such a strat-

egy is likely to have significant impact on their business. Yet a detailed and convoluted debate will be dismissed as being academic with little relevance to the 'real world'.

4. *Mindsets:* The topic of servitization sits at the confluence of two worldviews, production systems and service systems. It borrows ideas from each. An unfortunate consequence is that some people from the production systems world can struggle to envisage ambitious services offerings; similarly people from the service systems world can struggle to see value in products and technological competences.

History has a habit of repeating itself. In the early 1980s researchers were struggling to convey the virtues of Just-in-Time. The exemplars were from the automotive industry and companies like Toyota didn't stand out for profitability. *What was new anyway?* Inside a Toyota factory you will see many of the concepts pioneered by Henry Ford; standardized parts, division of labour and moving production lines. Perhaps only 20% of the way Toyota operated was significantly different. Through the late 1980s the language consolidated. Simple changes occurred, such as the word 'quality' generally being taken to refer to conformance to specification rather than inspiring a philosophical debate. In the early 1990s our knowledge of Just-in-Time consolidated, it translated into Lean, and today Toyota is the world's largest automotive manufacturer.

So, what was it those people just couldn't see in the 1980s? We've been through a paradigm shift in our ideas of how to organize design and production for efficient manufacture. As time moves on and the business environment continues to evolve, so too our ideas will continue to evolve; not abandoning those of the past but, just like Toyota, subsuming much of what has gone before. But make no mistake, as a community our knowledge base of servitization lags far behind that of Lean. Perhaps we are in the equivalent of the mid-1980s. This is not to suggest that it will take 30 years before the topic is mature and well understood, but rather that our knowledge base is fragile and will continue to evolve. This places a special challenge on you the reader.

We are in no doubt that servitization is vitally important. In carrying out the research for this book we have spent a large portion of our lives in the servitization world, but we also know well the world of production. In this book we set out to deliver the message that these worlds are different, and explain how and why this is. If you are deeply involved with production, maybe hold off for a moment from relating back to your own worldview. In return, we will set out to convey the principles, concepts, practices and technologies of servitization practically and succinctly. Our goal is for you to appreciate that this phenomenon is something subtle and not simply about adding a few services to products.

1.4 Navigating This Book

We have shaped this book to reflect how we expect senior executives from manufacturing firms will want to appraise servitization. This introduction provides the necessary foundation for the four principal parts, namely:

1. *Business context:* Factors that are influencing the adoption of servitization especially by western manufacturers.
2. *Competing through services:* The key elements of servitization and advanced services; what they look like in practice, and the motivations, risks and rewards explaining their appeal.
3. *Service delivery system:* How leading manufacturers organize their operations to successfully support the delivery of advanced services.

4. *Readiness to servitize:* The conditions that favour the take-up of servitization, both within sectors and individual businesses, and the factors that influence success.

Each part begins with a brief summary of the subsequent content. In the final chapter we reflect on the book as a whole and suggest how servitization may continue to evolve into the future.

Part 1
Business Context

In this first part we review the broader business environment supporting servitization. Processes of market-pull and technology-push are
interplaying to favour increasing servitization within those manufacturers based in industrialized nations. Five themes stand out. Here, we
consider each of these and take a look at evidence and arguments that
begin to explain a growing interest in servitization. In summary, we
reveal a picture where:

From an economic perspective:

- *Production is moving away from western industrialized nations.*

- *Competition from low-cost economies is intense and intensifying; labour
  rates are a fraction of those in the West while productivity is improving
  faster.*

- *Services and the aftermarket represent an alternative strategy; the installed
  base of products (those already in the field) is significant.*

- *The commercial benefits can be significant; profit margins for services are
  potentially 2–3 times greater than those for products.*

From an environmental perspective:

- *There are global concerns about population, resource exploitation and
  consumption.*

- *Developed economies can set an example by doing more with less.*

- *Services enable dematerialization (reducing embodied energy and materials) and can positively impact environmental sustainability.*

- *There are also opportunities to improve 'green' credentials through
  services.*

From a market and social perspective:

- *Desires for increased ownership, hyper-consumption and the disposable
  society can challenge servitization.*

- Traditional 'collective' services (e.g. launderettes and TV repair shops) have suffered and declined.

- Products and services, however, don't necessarily compete; rather products can create platforms for new services (e.g. Apple's iPad, iTunes and apps).

- Also many services already exist, but it's now the manufacturer who is offering to deliver these.

- Fundamentally, extent of services activities is directly linked to the wealth of an economy.

From a technology innovation perspective:

- Information and communication technologies enable many services.

- Technologies are accessible and affordable.

- To a large extent, it's simply a case of the manufacturer extending their ICT network into their products.

From a knowledge perspective:

- The idea that value is co-created with customers, rather than being embedded in products, is gaining traction.

- Differences between services and manufacturing operations are better understood.

- We are gaining insight into the organizational structures, principles and processes that can deliver effective and efficient product-centric services.

- There is growing recognition that product-centric services have the potential to create sustainable business models and reduce the impact of material and energy use on the environment.

- We need to look at service as a system of interacting parts that include people, technology and business.

Chapter 2

The strategies that organizations adopt are largely a reflection of their business environment. The genesis of Lean production, for example, is rooted in the business conditions prevailing in Japan in the 1950s and 1960s. At the outset we clearly need to understand the extent to which the conditions in the current business climate are indeed conducive to manufacturers competing increasingly through services.

Establishing a broad and fully embracing picture is difficult. Quite simply, business conditions differ from sector to sector, and to a lesser extent from company to company. There are, however, five themes that recur in discussions about servitization. These range from statistics about the physical environment, through to trends in knowledge production. Collectively these themes paint a picture of business conditions, against which the adoption of a servitization strategy appears to be a sensible response. In this chapter we examine these themes and the arguments they offer.

First, a word on scope. Here, our focus is exclusively on the external business environment at a macro-level. We will avoid discussing the particular motives of individual organizations, or the benefits that have resulted from their strategies. These internal factors will be explored separately in Chapters 4 and 5.

2.1 An Economic Perspective

Over recent decades the economic centre of gravity for production has been steadily shifting away from the (mainly western) leading industrialized nations. In the USA, for example, growth has dropped from an average annual rate of 7% in the 1960s to 4.2% in 2010.[1] Figure 2.1 shows how the world's principal economies are currently aligned and how they are expected to change in the foreseeable future.

In this global picture emergent economies are expected to expand significantly. China, for example, is predicted to overtake the USA as the 'world's largest economy' by 2025.[2] Others will also push ahead. Although markets for new product offerings will remain substantial in Europe and North America, they will no longer expand at the rate that they once were.

At the level of individual industries the picture is complex and there are mixed fortunes for western manufacturers. For instance, the value of output of the USA's pottery, ceramics and plumbing fixture manufacturing industry almost halved between 2000 and 2010 (from $4bn to $2.1bn), while that of the mining and oil and gas field machinery manufacturing industry more than doubled (from $7.4bn to $18.5bn over the same period).[3]

[1] US Department for Commerce, Bureau of Economic Analysis, http://www.bea.gov/industry/gdpbyind_data.htm
[2] PWC, referenced in The Guardian data blog, January 2011.
[3] US Bureau of Economic Analysis, 2011.

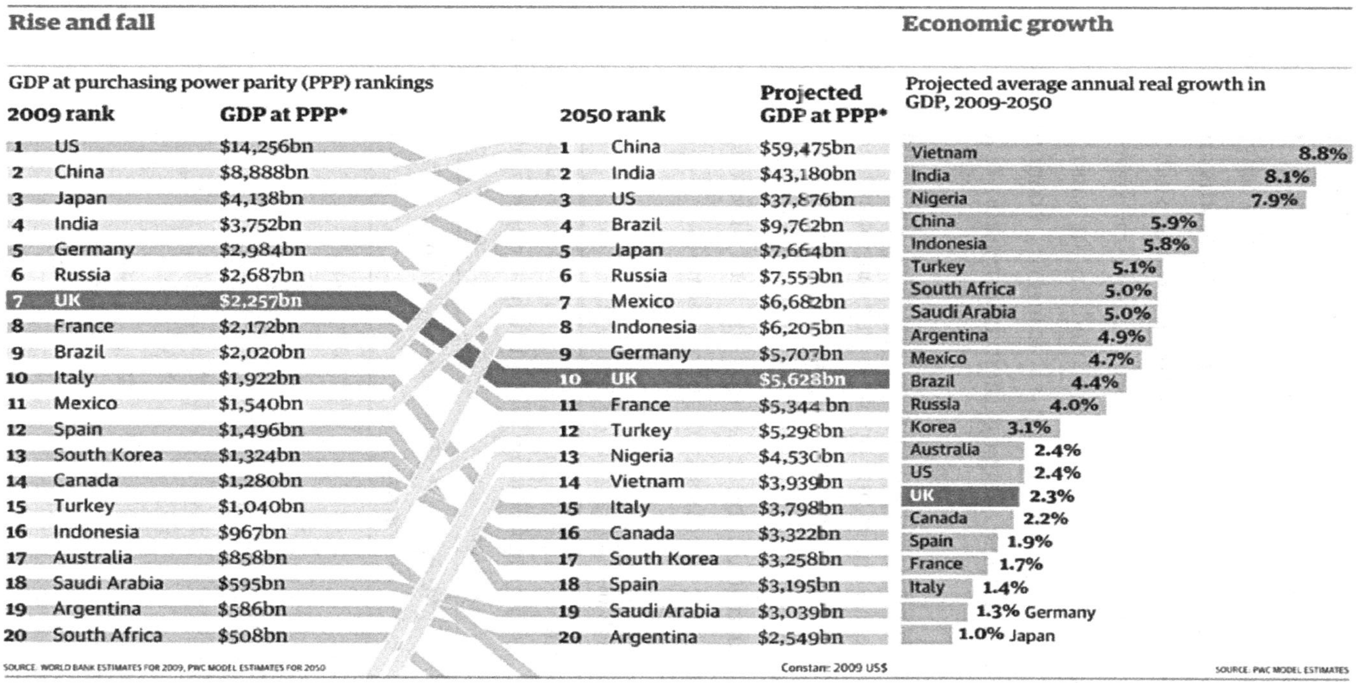

Rise and fall

GDP at purchasing power parity (PPP) rankings

2009 rank	GDP at PPP*	2050 rank	Projected GDP at PPP*
1 US	$14,256bn	1 China	$59,475bn
2 China	$8,888bn	2 India	$43,180bn
3 Japan	$4,138bn	3 US	$37,876bn
4 India	$3,752bn	4 Brazil	$9,762bn
5 Germany	$2,984bn	5 Japan	$7,664bn
6 Russia	$2,687bn	6 Russia	$7,559bn
7 UK	$2,257bn	7 Mexico	$6,682bn
8 France	$2,172bn	8 Indonesia	$6,205bn
9 Brazil	$2,020bn	9 Germany	$5,707bn
10 Italy	$1,922bn	10 UK	$5,628bn
11 Mexico	$1,540bn	11 France	$5,344 bn
12 Spain	$1,496bn	12 Turkey	$5,298bn
13 South Korea	$1,324bn	13 Nigeria	$4,530bn
14 Canada	$1,280bn	14 Vietnam	$3,939bn
15 Turkey	$1,040bn	15 Italy	$3,798bn
16 Indonesia	$967bn	16 Canada	$3,322bn
17 Australia	$858bn	17 South Korea	$3,258bn
18 Saudi Arabia	$595bn	18 Spain	$3,195bn
19 Argentina	$586bn	19 Saudi Arabia	$3,039bn
20 South Africa	$508bn	20 Argentina	$2,549bn

SOURCE: WORLD BANK ESTIMATES FOR 2009, PWC MODEL ESTIMATES FOR 2050

Constant: 2009 US$

Economic growth

Projected average annual real growth in GDP, 2009–2050

Vietnam	8.8%
India	8.1%
Nigeria	7.9%
China	5.9%
Indonesia	5.8%
Turkey	5.1%
South Africa	5.0%
Saudi Arabia	5.0%
Argentina	4.9%
Mexico	4.7%
Brazil	4.4%
Russia	4.0%
Korea	3.1%
Australia	2.4%
US	2.4%
UK	2.3%
Canada	2.2%
Spain	1.9%
France	1.7%
Italy	1.4%
Germany	1.3%
Japan	1.0%

SOURCE: PWC MODEL ESTIMATES

Figure 2.1: *Possible scenario for the re-ranking of the world's economies*[4]
(*Source: The Guardian data blog/PWC, January 2011*)

[4] http://www.guardian.co.uk/news/datablog/2011/jan/07/gdp-projections-china-us-uk-brazil; *Purchasing Power Parity

Least affected are those industries where product 'identity' is closely associated with a particular country or region. The brand values of Harley Davidson Motorcycles are intrinsically linked to manufacture in the USA, and the same is true for Lotus and Morgan cars in the UK. Similarly there are some products, such as nuclear medicines, that have an extremely short shelf-life and have to be produced in the same location as they are used. In the same way some products are too large and heavy to transport economically, or there may be regulations affecting their importation (e.g. military aerospace).

Other industries are more exposed. Many of the emerging economic powers were simply not open as international traders in the 1960s; it was only in the 1990s that countries such as China, India and Brazil began to compete seriously. Their competitive advantages are significant. To illustrate, Table 2.1 shows the vast differences in rates of pay and output for a cross-section of economies.

Table 2.1 The growth in international competition

Country	Hourly compensation costs in manufacturing in USD		Increase in output per manufacturing employee (index, 2002 = 100)		
	2010	% change (USD) since 1997	1997	2010	% change in output since 1997
USA	34.74	3.2	76.1	149.8	197
UK	29.44	3.6	83.1	128	154
Germany	43.76	3.2	90.5	112.9	125
France	40.55	3.8	88.4	120.9	137
China*	1.36	2.19	NA	NA	NA
India*	2.3	1.44	NA	NA	NA
Singapore	19.10	3.5	78.4	143.7	183
Taiwan	NA	NA	78.7	176.9	225
PR Korea	NA	NA	66	160.7	243
Japan	NA	NA	91.5	134.9	147

(Source: US Bureau of Labor Statistics, 2011); *Estimates

The differences in labour rates are substantial. Employee costs in China, for example, are only 4% of those in the USA, while employee costs in India are only 8% of those in the UK. Most worryingly for western manufacturers, the trend is for these gaps gaps to widen in the near future. In China, rates are only increasing at 70% of those in the USA, and for India this is 40% of those in the UK.

Emergent economies are also sustaining productivity improvements. Table 2.1 shows how the output per employee in Taiwan, Korea and Singapore is improving faster than that of the UK, Germany and France. Of western manufacturers only the USA comes close to matching the productivity improvements of emergent economies.

A frequent response to such data is to suggest that western manufacturers can compete by focusing on higher-value products. Intriguingly, this was the strategy of the British motorcycle industry in the late 1960s and early 1970s, which subsequently disappeared as Japanese competitors also followed this strategy. Nevertheless, as Figure 2.2 illustrates, the USA is, for the moment, managing to sustain such a strategy.

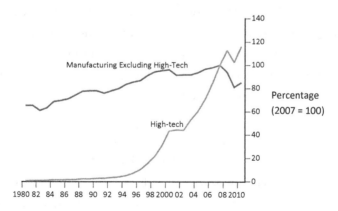

Figure 2.2: *High-technology manufacturing versus production excluding high-technology in the USA*
(Source: US Department of Commerce, January 2012)[5]

[5] 'The Competitiveness and Innovative Capacity of the United States', page 6-5.

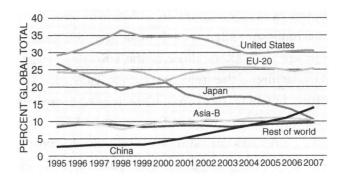

Figure 2.3: *High-technology manufacturing value-added share by country/economy:*
1995–2007
(Source: National Science Foundation, 2010)[6]

Not surprisingly the emerging economies are following a similar strategy. Initially they favoured producing high volumes of less complex products, but then they set about developing capabilities to produce higher quality products. This is illustrated by comparing the changing share of medium–high tech exports by country in the world market (Figure 2.3).

A rather bleak picture therefore emerges for western companies competing on the basis of new product sales alone, especially for low-tech products with a high-labour content and long shelf-life, and which are easily imported. Taking this challenge head-on requires radical new product innovation and aggressive cost reduction programmes. In some industries this is viable.

Many new opportunities for sales are also opening up as lower-cost economies themselves become richer. Demand is rising for niche western products with high-brand values. For example, luxury car manufacturers such as BMW and Mercedes are experiencing significant growth in China's markets. By 2015, it is projected that demand

[6] http://www.nsf.gov/statistics/seind10/tables.htm

for luxury cars in China will surge to 800,000 cars annually.[7] Yet for those without strong brands the situation is more concerning.

Exploitation of services and the aftermarket is an alternative strategy. The extent of the opportunity is driven by the size of the 'installed product base'. This term refers to the number of products that are out in the field and is typically an order of magnitude greater than the number of products sold annually. Take the United States as an illustration. The number of automobiles sold in 2009 was 5.4 million vehicles,[8] yet the total number of registered vehicles was 134.9 million[9] – a ratio of 25:1. In other words, for every new vehicle sale, 25 were already in use.

Evidence is growing around the economic benefits to manufacturers of servicing this installed base. An indication of this opportunity is illustrated in Table 2.2. This shows how the profit margin for services

Table 2.2 Illustrating a potential opportunity for profit from services in 2010

Industry	Margin in product manufacture	Margin in services	Margin leverage (service/product)
Paper machines	3.4%	13.1%	3.8
Power equipment	7%	9.9%	1.4
Instruments	4.9%	12.3%	2.5
Machine tools	5.3%	8.9%	1.67
Rail	6.3%	12.6%	2

(Source: http://money.cnn.com/magazines/fortune/fortune500/2009/performers/industries/profits/ (10 January 2010))

[7] http://www.etftrends.com/2010/07/consumer-etfs-going-global-find-strength/ referenced in BIS Economics Paper 10A (op cit).

[8] US Bureau of Transportation, National Transportation Statistics – http://www.bts.gov/publications/national_transportation_statistics/ (11 January 2011).

[9] US Bureau of Transport National Transportation Statistics – http://www.bts.gov/publications/state_transportation_statistics/state_transportation_statistics_2010/html/fast_facts.html (11 January 2012).

is presently higher than for products in many industries. Again, such general statistics are fraught with limitations, but evidence is growing that services are a sound business proposition for manufacturers.

Recent studies in the UK reinforce this evidence. They show that of manufacturers adding a service proposition to their offerings, the majority of businesses (almost 60%) report revenue growth over the last five years. Indeed, 24% reported an increase of between 25% and 50%.[10] Similar indications are apparent in the USA, Finland, and Singapore.

A move into services is not a panacea and improvements in profits are not automatic. Much depends on the type of services being offered, the extent to which product and service innovation is complementary, and the capabilities that the manufacturer has in place to deliver such services. We will explore these topics further in the following chapters.

To summarize this economic perspective; in western economies especially, new product sales are tending to reduce and competition for those sales is increasing. Yet the installed base of products is high, and the potential profitability in servicing these is significant. It's not surprising, therefore, that policy makers in developed economies are encouraging manufacturers to explore servitization.

2.2 An Environmental Perspective

At the outset of our programme two research communities stood out. The first consisted of researchers, mainly from the USA, who looked to servitization for the economic potential as discussed above. The second was the product–service systems (PSS) community, largely from Scandinavia, who looked to servitization largely for its potential benefits to environmental sustainability.

[10] Barclays Corporate 'Servitisation and the Future of UK Manufacturing: The power to help you succeed' (September 2011).

Table 2.3 Population growth[11]

Country	Estimated population at constant fertility rates, millions	
	2010	2030
USA	310	361
UK	62	69
Germany	82	77
France	62	68
Brazil	194	227
India	1224	1610
China	1341	1407
World	6895.9	8700.3

(Source. United Nations)

The environmental argument is based on the premise that current patterns of human activity cannot be sustained. The current global situation is characterized by three critical trends:

- Overpopulation and continuing population growth, especially in developing countries.

- Accelerating resource exploitation, shortages and increasing pollution levels.[12]

- A need to reduce poverty and to improve living standards in the underdeveloped countries.

The extent of the challenge is illustrated by reflecting on expected population growth (Table 2.3). The United Nations predicts that world

[11] http://data.un.org/Data.aspx?d=PopDiv&f=variableID%3a12 (10 January 2010).
[12] E.g. copper, platinum – Scientific American, 'Measure of Metal Supply Finds Future Shortage' by David Biello, 17 January 2006; and Bloomberg (2011) – http://www.bloomberg.com/news/2011-09-05/copper-may-have-shortage-for-third-year-on-china-demand-pan-pacific-says.html

population will grow from 6.9 billion in 2010 to 8.7 billion by 2030. This population growth, combined with increasing standards of living for many people in developing countries, will cause strong growth in energy demand.

The global situation with energy consumption is captured in Figure 2.4. Demand will increase by one-third from 2010 to 2035, with China and India accounting for 50% of the growth[13] – currently some two billion people have no access to electricity. By 2035, China will consume nearly 70% more energy than the United States. Even then, the energy consumption per capita in China will still be less than half the level in the United States. The rates of growth in energy consumption in India, Indonesia, Brazil and the Middle East are forecast to be even faster than in China.

Over the same period, energy-related CO_2 outputs could increase by 20%. Much depends on the speed at which industries are legislated. Figure 2.5 illustrates that the longer it takes for action to be taken, then

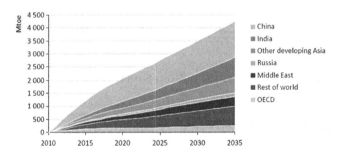

Figure 2.4: *Projected growth in energy demand (Mtoe = Million tonnes of oil equivalent)*
Source: International Energy Agency, 2011[14]

[13] International Energy Agency – World Energy Outlook 2011 – presentation and factsheets: http://www.worldenergyoutlook.org/docs/weo2011/homepage/WEO2011_Press_Launch_London.pdf

[14] World Energy Outlook 2011, Presentation to the press (London, 9 November 2011).

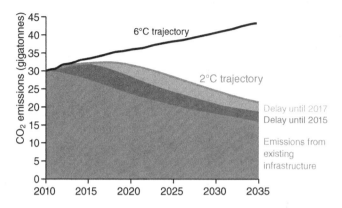

Figure 2.5: *Projected growth CO2 emissions and global warming (Note: 6°C/2°C trajectory refers to worst case/best case scenarios for global warming by 2035) (Source: International Energy Agency, 2010[14])*

the greater the burden of power plants, factories, buildings, etc., that simply don't comply with regulations. This will inevitably push forwards the extent of global warming.

Excessive demands on resources are linked directly to trends in consumption. Our ideas of wealth, lifestyle, personal development and economic prosperity are built upon an excessive use of non-renewable energy and natural resources.

Scandinavian researchers emphasize that this is compounded by a willingness of people to accept ecological degradation in exchange for a small and short increase in economic and personal well-being. They highlight how developing countries, in particular, will exploit all forms of opportunities to tip the present economic unbalance in their favour. The consequence is an acceleration of the destructive competition for resources.

The challenge for developed economies is to set an example by doing more with less. Unfortunately consumption is prolific. Table 2.4 illustrates as an example the trend for increasing ownership in the United States, impacting on all kinds of unsustainable resource

Table 2.4 Consumer durable ownership in USA (measured in terms of billions of dollars)

	Line	1997	1998	1999	2000	2001	2002	2003	2004	2005	2006	2007	2008	2009	2010
Consumer durable goods	1	**2,720.9**	**2,837.0**	**2,996.2**	**3,196.0**	**3,359.4**	**3,524.7**	**3,682.0**	**3,894.1**	**4,098.0**	**4,293.6**	**4,468.3**	**4,566.8**	**4,571.6**	**4,581.8**
Motor vehicles and parts	2	**870.9**	**917.1**	**980.2**	**1,041.5**	**1,105.2**	**1,162.0**	**1,210.4**	**1,268.4**	**1,302.1**	**1,305.9**	**1,317.5**	**1,260.5**	**1,274.2**	**1,262.6**
Autos	3	500.2	505.2	518.2	536.2	547.8	547.6	540.8	544.9	553.9	557.0	552.0	540.3	532.2	511.8
Light trucks	4	362.2	403.2	452.9	495.9	548.0	604.9	660.0	713.6	737.7	737.9	754.1	708.6	731.0	739.6
Motor vehicle parts and accessories	5	8.5	8.7	9.0	9.4	9.4	9.5	9.5	9.9	10.4	11.0	11.4	11.6	11.0	11.2
Furnishings and durable household equipment	6	**845.6**	**882.2**	**923.0**	**977.4**	**1,015.8**	**1,062.2**	**1,100.7**	**1,170.4**	**1,242.4**	**1,317.1**	**1,364.7**	**1,414.7**	**1,396.6**	**1,372.6**
Furniture and furnishings[1]	7	517.7	544.2	569.8	604.6	624.3	655.1	678.1	718.5	760.6	806.6	830.2	859.0	850.9	834.3
Household appliances[2]	8	145.8	147.9	153.4	159.4	168.8	175.0	177.8	186.9	204.7	221.7	231.5	242.4	234.7	227.3
Glassware, tableware, and household utensils[3]	9	117.7	124.5	130.0	139.4	145.7	152.6	161.5	174.3	179.3	184.8	196.1	203.4	202.7	202.6
Tools and equipment for house and garden	10	64.4	65.6	69.8	74.0	77.0	79.5	83.3	90.7	97.9	104.0	107.0	109.9	108.3	108.4
Recreational goods and vehicles	11	**602.3**	**631.7**	**668.8**	**727.8**	**771.7**	**820.3**	**867.7**	**923.8**	**985.9**	**1,033.6**	**1,086.4**	**1,136.8**	**1,119.9**	**1,125.3**
Video, audio, photographic, and information processing equipment and media	12	272.0	283.4	300.8	328.9	345.0	367.8	388.2	417.4	445.8	462.9	489.7	502.2	489.9	501.1

Sporting equipment, supplies, guns, and ammunition	13	128.3	130.9	135.3	146.3	156.4	167.4	181.7	190.8	204.5	217.3	230.0	256.3	255.1	253.0
Sports and recreational vehicles[4]	14	104.8	113.1	122.9	134.3	141.9	148.7	156.0	167.3	182.7	194.4	200.9	205.4	200.4	195.3
Recreational books	15	84.6	91.0	95.4	102.2	110.6	117.5	121.8	127.0	131.0	136.2	142.4	148.6	150.0	151.8
Musical instruments	16	12.6	13.4	14.4	16.2	17.7	19.0	19.9	21.2	22.0	22.9	23.5	24.4	24.6	24.1
Other durable goods	17	**402.1**	**405.9**	**424.2**	**449.4**	**466.9**	**480.2**	**503.3**	**531.5**	**567.6**	**636.9**	**699.8**	**754.7**	**780.9**	**821.3**
Jewelry and watches	18	191.6	195.3	205.4	219.2	226.5	230.3	239.3	254.1	268.7	301.8	330.7	355.9	360.1	382.0
Therapeutic appliances and equipment	19	70.8	75.9	82.1	88.7	92.8	96.3	101.9	108.5	117.1	125.0	134.6	141.1	146.5	153.7
Educational books	20	40.1	42.7	45.0	48.8	52.2	55.7	58.5	61.0	64.8	69.6	74.9	79.4	82.9	84.2
Luggage and similar personal items	21	83.1	76.0	75.6	75.9	77.4	79.0	82.9	84.3	90.6	110.2	123.8	136.8	145.6	151.9
Telephone and facsimile equipment	22	16.4	16.2	16.1	16.8	17.9	18.9	20.6	23.6	26.4	30.3	35.7	41.5	45.9	49.5

[1.] Consists of furniture, clocks, lamps, lighting fixtures, and other household decorative items, carpets and other floor coverings, and window coverings.

[2.] Consists of major household appliances and small electric household appliances, except built-in appliances, which are classified as part of residential structures.

[3.] Consists of dishes, flatware, and non-electric cookware and tableware.

[4.] Consists of motorcycles, bicycles and accessories, and pleasure boats, aircraft, and other recreational vehicles.

(Source: http://numbrary.com/sources/d79390ddbf-table-13-current-net (10 January 2010)) consumption. To take an example, an average car today is lighter, more fuel efficient, and emits less pollution per kilometre travelled than a car from the mid-1970s. But, the total number of cars has increased to an extent that these technical achievements have been outweighed. Today, transport accounts for up to 70% of all CO_2 emissions.

Various concepts have emerged to help address these issues. Some advocate naturalistic approaches, others suggest dematerialization of present economies and eco-efficiency. Eco-efficiency is largely a technological solution, and based on the premise that societies can largely continue to behave as they have if they do everything much better. Dematerialization refers to the absolute or relative reduction in the quantity of materials required to service the economic functions in society.

Servitization is conducive to dematerialization. It encourages manufacturers to be more responsible for their products and engaging directly with services such as take-back, recycling and refurbishment. Consequently, it encourages them to use their technical knowledge to find ways to deliver the same 'outcome' from a product while using less energy and material, and so reduce cost and environmental impact. Xerox illustrates how this can occur in practice. Through their managed print services they have helped Fiat Group to reduce print operations costs by an estimated 30%, and also assisted its sustainability agenda by reducing energy use by up to 50%.

The resulting green credentials are themselves valuable to the associated organization. Companies that are pursuing environmentally and ethically friendly strategies may well offer significant strategic opportunity for the wider economy in the longer term. Many opportunities exist for companies to gain competitive advantage through such green credentials. As society becomes increasingly concerned with environmental issues, those companies with more adventurous 'green' strategies are likely to be leaders in the development of new products and businesses opportunities and will have excellent growth potential.

2.3 A Market and Social Perspective

Servitization offers economic and environmental benefits, but are consumers ready to abandon products and ownership in favour of services?

As people we appear to have strong desires to own, possess and consume. Ownership provides more than simply utility of a particular product. It is widely seen as a vehicle for reinforcing an individual's identity, expressing values, or stressing an affiliation with a particular group or lifestyle. Product ownership also provides the consumer freedom to customize products as they wish, and gives them the rights to control use. For some, ownership is also a form of compensation for their perceived inadequacies. They accumulate and use products in order to expand their sense of control over their environment and increase their perceived power.

The urge to own an increasing number of objects results in 'hyper-consumption', in which the division between needs and wants becomes progressively blurred. This can be fuelled by advertising and the media. A partial consequence of this is a move towards cheaper, less durable products. This is accompanied by a gradual acceptance of disposability, and a stigma attached to second-hand products, repair and thrifty behaviour.

Hyper-consumption is also fuelled by ever-increasing manufacturing productivity keeping costs down, and the influx of cheaper goods from emerging economies. As an example: from 2001 each year sales of footwear and clothing in the UK have risen sometimes by as much as 12%. Yet from 2003 to 2007 average prices have fallen by 10%, and the trend continues. Quite simply we are buying more and spending less (*Sunday Observer*, 8 May 2011).

These demands for ownership have an adverse impact upon some services. Where product ownership has risen, there has been a corresponding decline in the number of products under rental agreements and the amount of repair work undertaken, especially for low-tech, low-risk products in the business-to-consumer sectors. Also, many products are simply more reliable and require less maintenance than they once did. Finally, some traditional 'collective' services have been supplemented by personally owned labour-saving appliances; the movement away from launderette to washing machine, from cinema to television, from train to car and so on.

On the other hand, the growth of innovative services through digital technology is becoming increasingly significant in the development of the economy. The improved communication provided by such technology enables the rapid transmission of data and offers new opportunities for service innovations such as telephone and internet banking.

Additionally, the services that manufacturers offer with servitization are not necessarily new innovations. Frequently, these services are already being carried out either by competitors (via pure-service providers) or the customers themselves (via their own operations).

Indeed, the extent of services business activity within an economy can be directly linked to wealth. Figure 2.6 illustrates the relationship between Gross Domestic Product per Capita and the share of employment in business services across European states. This helps to illustrate that as the business services sector develops, the average income in an economy goes up. Such evidence shows both the opportunity of services in developed economies and helps to explain why less developed economies look to develop services sectors.

All this goes to show that products and services don't necessarily compete. The desire for ownership does have an adverse effect upon

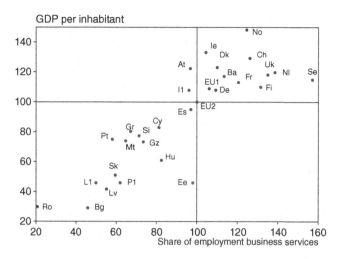

Figure 2.6: *Correlation between GDP per capita and the share of business service in total employment*
(Source: Ecorys Research & Consulting/2008[15])

some services, but this also brings opportunities for others. Most telling, developed economies are services-based demonstrating that markets for services are significant. One way or another, society is increasing its appetite for services.

2.4 A Technology Innovation Perspective

So far we have examined the 'pull' for services. Economic, environmental, market and social factors that all indicate opportunities for the services that manufacturers can provide. Here, and in the following section, we take a 'push' perspective. We explore the development of technologies and knowledge that is equipping manufacturers to exploit this opportunity.

---

[15] 'Study on Industrial Policy & Services' for the European Commission.

Information and communication technologies (ICTs) are key enablers of servitization. Leading manufacturers are developing significant ICT capabilities that give them information about the 'visability'
of their products in the field – in particular, where they are located,
how they are being used, and their condition and performance. We
explore such systems in detail in Chapter 8.

Here, we simply set out to illustrate broadly how the world of ICTs
is rapidly evolving. In doing so, we show that the relevant ICT capabilities, demanded by servitization, are becoming readily accessible to
many manufacturers. In particular, that the step-up in technology
knowledge is not too dissimilar to that needed during the implementa-
tion of computerized production planning systems. To a large extent,
the manufacturer is simply extending their ICT network into their
products to monitor how they are used and how they perform.

Sophisticated services often require ICT to 'sense' products. These
sensing or monitoring parameters vary to reflect the form of the
service offering. For example, a services contract that guarantees reliability of a Rolls-Royce aircraft engine may require bearing vibration
data, whereas an offering focusing on the economy of a MAN truck
may require data from the fuel pump.

The accessibility of such sensing technologies is exemplified by the
readiness of Global Navigation Satellite Systems (GNSS). GNSS can
be used to locate vehicles (e.g. trucks, buses, police cars, taxis) in order
to optimize resource management, reduce travel time, increase secu-
rity and reduce fuel consumption. In 2009 the number of vehicles
equipped with fleet management and vehicle tracking systems was six
million in North America and roughly five million in the EU. Almost
30% of road vehicles in the EU have a GNSS device on board and 22%
worldwide.

The rate at which these GNSS technologies have become available
is illustrated in Figure 2.7. The average growth over the past five years
has been over 60%, much of which has been in Europe and North

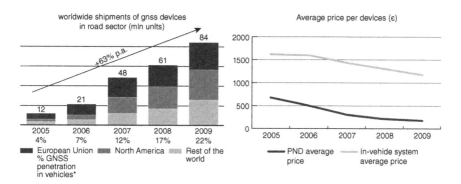

Figure 2.7: *Indicating the accessibility of ICT capabilities: availability and pricing of GNSS*

(Source: European GNSS Agency, 2010[16])

America. These are the very markets that many manufacturers would target with servitization. The average price of such units has also decreased significantly. In 2009 this was less than 500 Euro, and the trend continues downwards.

In addition, the ICT capabilities associated with sophisticated services often require a wide array of microprocessor technologies. These may be within on-board sensors, or used in the localized analysis and recording of faults, making the acquisition, communication and storage of data on a product relatively straightforward. Similarly they may be applied to analyse the data at the manufacturer's home, helping to turn this into information that facilitates effective service delivery.

Again the price/performance ratios are increasingly attractive. Figure 2.8 uses Moore's law to illustrate the increasing affordability of microprocessor technologies. Intriguingly, charts such as this were readily available during the 1990s and early 2000s. More up-to-date ones are elusive. *Why is this?* The cost of these technologies is simply no longer the issue that it once was.

[16] www.gsa.europa.eu

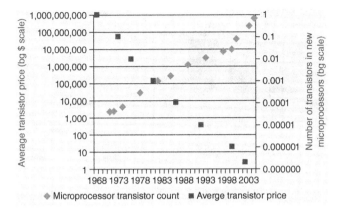

Figure 2.8: *Moore's law and the affordability of powerful computing*
(Source: Intel/BERR Economics Paper 2, 2008)

The technologies in Figures 2.7 and 2.8 are only examples of the increasing accessibility of ICT. They paint only part of the picture. We could have given similar evidence for information transaction rates, or the penetration of the internet into the workplace. The message is quite simple. ICT capabilities are available, accessible and affordable.

2.5 A Knowledge Perspective

Our knowledge of servitization has evolved significantly in recent years. While there is still much to be learnt, there is now a burgeoning research base that manufacturers can call upon for insight into servitization and related topics. In this section we take a look at this knowledge base.

Five research communities have been especially active in this broad area, these are:

- Services marketing.

- Service management.

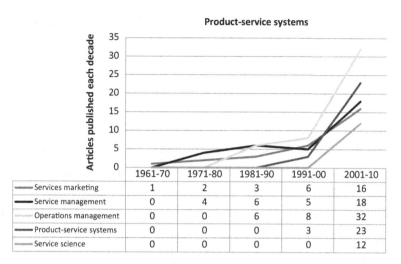

	1961-70	1971-80	1981-90	1991-00	2001-10
Services marketing	1	2	3	6	16
Service management	0	4	6	5	18
Operations management	0	0	6	8	32
Product-service systems	0	0	0	3	23
Service science	0	0	0	0	12

Figure 2.9: *Growth of research outputs contributing to the knowledge of servitization*

- Operations management.

- Product–service systems.

- Service science.

Collectively these span the disciplines of engineering and management, though they do tend to operate rather independently. The extent of their activities is indicated by the number of articles that they have published in research journals. Figure 2.9 illustrates this, and shows how research outputs have increased significantly from the 1960s through to the present day.

Overall our knowledge of servitization is still relatively modest. By comparison, the number of articles associated with 'Lean techniques in manufacturing' is an order of magnitude higher. Nevertheless the knowledge base is growing actively. We will now take a closer look at the origin of key contributions, and insights emerging from each of these five communities.

Services marketing community

Services marketing is a subset of the more traditional marketing community. It reflects a change in emphasis, from the exchange and distribution of commodities, to a focus on customer relationship management in the provision of services.

The first issue of the *Journal of Marketing* was published in 1936. This included a review by Howard Taylor of the research existing at that time, and in this he noted a focus on the exchange and distribution of commodities. It was only in the late 1970s that Glynne Shostack heralded an acknowledgement that the marketing of services was different to products.

Initially the marketing of goods and services was seen as different. Services were characterized as intangible, heterogeneous, inseparable and perishable (IHIP). In the early 2000s this idea was challenged. Researchers such as Chris Lovelock and Evert Gummesson identified shortcomings in the IHIP concept. They suggest that exchanges not resulting in the transfer of ownership from seller to buyer are fundamentally different from those that do. Also, that service provision offers benefits through access or temporary possession, not simply ownership.

At the same time a new service-centred dominant logic was being proposed by Steve Vargo and Bob Lusch. They introduced the notion that value is co-created with the customer rather than embedded in output. This service-dominant logic (SDL) marketing paradigm argues that all of marketing research and practice must break free from the manufacturing-based model of exchange of output. Not all marketing professionals necessarily accept this view, but it is clearly an alternative perspective on marketing to that of the 1930s.

Services management community

The services management researchers have largely evolved from mainstream operations and strategy domains and tend to focus on the organization of service-based businesses and industries.

They began to coalesce around the late 1960s to recognize the importance of services to the economic output of many nations. A key milestone was in 1976 when Theodore Levitt produced a paper titled 'The Industrialisation of Services' where he pointed out that the service sector of industrialized nations had been in the ascent for almost three-quarters of a century. Simultaneously, Earl Sasser argued that immediacy makes service industries distinct from manufacturing.

During the 1980s services management established its own identity. Researchers such as Dick Chase and David Garvin introduced the 'Service Factory' concept. These contributions helped establish that operations that are appropriate for delivering services differ from those associated with more traditional manufacturing. This argument still stands. In 2007 Janelle Heineke and Mark Davis noted that applying manufacturing operations management concepts to service operations is limiting.

Our own research clearly supports this view. As later chapters of this book illustrate, the operations that support servitization differ markedly to those of production.

Servitization community

This is largely a group of researchers, within the wider operations management community, that have chosen to focus their work on helping manufacturers to compete through services. The origins of this work lie principally in North America in the late 1980s. Authors such as Sandra Vandermerwe, Juan Rada, Richard Wise and Peter Baumgartner heralded servitization, the underlying motive being that services were a key opportunity for manufacturers to build their revenue streams and deliver value-add by moving downstream towards their customers' area of business activity.

Since then there has been a growing number of articles and papers addressing the 'servitization of manufacturing'. The focus has largely been on product-centric services, where the manufactured product itself is central to the provision of an integrated set of services (e.g. through maintenance, repair, support, availability and capability contracts). Examples given frequently include Xerox's move from selling printers and copiers to delivering a 'Document Management Service' and Rolls-Royce Civil Aerospace's 'TotalCare' service.

In more recent years researchers in the UK have driven forwards our understanding of servitization. Andy Neely has helped to establish a much better understanding of the relationships between the adoption of services and economic success. Duncan McFarlane and Irene Ng have led consortia based out of Cambridge University to study the complexities of service delivery networks in manufacturing. Mark Johnson, Raj Roy, Steve Evans, and their colleagues at Cranfield University have sought to help manufacturers to design and manage product–service systems. Important contributions have also been made by Advanced Institute of Management scholars such as Martin Spring, Chris Voss and Veronica Martinez.

Product–service systems community

The product–service systems (PSS) community has largely originated from Scandinavia and northern Europe. This is a relatively recent body of research that sets out to improve social, economic and environmental and industrial sustainability.

The foundational work on PSS is exemplified by Mark Goedkoop's report in 1999 on the ecological and economic basis (commissioned by VROM and EZ in Holland) and Oksana Mont in 2000 (sponsored by the Swedish Waste Research Council). Since then various models and tools have been developed to help organizations to adopt PSS. Examples include the product–service spectrum and product–service development toolkit that can be found in Arnold Tukker and Ursula Tischner's book *New Business for Old Europe*, which discusses product–service development, competitiveness and sustainability.

A diverse range of PSS examples can be found in academic literature. Some of these demonstrate economic success, but most tend to emphasize the potential for significant environmental and social gains. Industrial PSS (IPS2) is a developing subset of PSS which focuses especially on business-to-business solutions. Although developed in unconnected research streams and coming from different points of departure, there is a striking overlap in concepts within the servitization and PSS communities.

Service science community

The service science perspective has evolved largely from information systems (IS). It is a relatively new initiative that promotes interdisciplinary working to provide a better understanding of complex service systems. Fostered mainly within IBM, a service system is seen as a melding of activities that include people, technology and business. As such it draws on ideas and concepts from a wide range of disciplines including computer science, engineering, cognitive science, economics, organizational behaviour, human resources management, marketing and operations research.

Service science has become a fast-developing research theme. At the first International Symposium on Service Science in 2009 research on a variety of topics was presented from both academic and practitioner viewpoints. These included the modelling of service systems, services and customer orientation, service engineering, service-oriented software structures and hybrid products and services.

Table 2.5 Overview of contributions being made to our knowledge of servitization

Community	Has contributed to our understanding around:
Services marketing	Value being co-created with customer rather than embedded in products
Service management	Service operations differ in their configuration to manufacturing operations
Operations management	Establishing the organizational structures, principles and processes that can deliver effective and efficient product-centric services
Product–service systems	Product-centric services have the potential to create sustainable business models and reduce the impact of material and energy use on the environment
Service science	Applying a focus on service as a system of interacting parts that include products, people, technology and business

Summarizing the knowledge base

Our summary of these five research communities simply represents a snapshot in their development. Table 2.5 captures, in brief, how these communities are contributing to our understanding of servitization.

The picture is still evolving. Although Figure 2.9 shows that growth has accelerated rapidly in recent years, how this may continue into the future is somewhat uncertain. In some areas enthusiasm has waned as researchers discover new directions while in others activity has intensified.

New communities are emerging and links to existing communities are strengthening. This is especially the case with the technology communities. Condition monitoring and remote product sensing have been active research topics for some time, but there is now much interest in their role in supporting servitization. Particular topics include Integrated Vehicle Health Management (IVHM),

Prognostics and Health Management (PHM) strategy, and Condition-based Maintenance (CBM).

Links are also clearer to research in supply chain, vertical integration and outsourcing. Indeed, researchers such as Roger Schmener suggest that servitization is a special case in outsourcing/vertical integration. They see manufacturers as moving forwards in their supply chains to become providers in an outsourcing relationship with the customer.

2.6 Summarizing the Business Context

Innovations come about through an interplay of market-pull and technology-push. In this chapter we have examined five sets of factors that reflect this interplay in the case of servitization. The picture is broad and complex. Some manufacturers will inevitably succeed through product innovation, aggressive cost reduction programmes and exploitation of international supply chains. For others the arguments supporting servitization are compelling.

Servitization is conducive to economic sustainability. Production is moving away from western industrialized nations. The competition from low-cost economies is intense and intensifying, with labour rates being only a fraction of those in the West while productivity is improving faster. Services and the aftermarket represent an alternative strategy. The extent of the market is represented by the size of the installed base of products which, in developed economies, is often many times the annual sale of new products. The commercial benefits of servicing this installed base can be significant; revenue and profit margins for services can be 2–3 times greater than those for products.

Servitization is conducive to environmental sustainability. There are global concerns about population, resource exploitation and consumption. Developed economies can set an example by doing more with less, and services are a way of demonstrating this. Services enable dematerialization (reducing embodied energy and materials) and can impact positively upon environmental sustainability. There are also opportunities for manufacturers to differentiate themselves through the 'green' credentials they can generate through service.

Market and social demand for services is strong. Products and services don't necessarily compete; rather products can create platforms for new services (e.g. Apple's iPad, iTunes and apps). Moreover, many services already exist, it's simply a case that the manufacturer is well positioned to deliver these.

Technological innovations needed to support servitization are already in place. The technological barriers are frequently much lower than expected and, to a large extent, it's simply a case of the manufacturer extending their ICT network into their products.

Our knowledge of how to compete through servitization is strengthening. Ideas that value is co-created with customers rather than embedded in products are gaining traction. Also, the differences between services and manufacturing operations are better understood, with increasing insight into the organizational structures, principles and processes that can deliver effective and efficient product-centric services.

Our conclusion from this is that it's hard to imagine why any manufacturer should ignore exploring some aspect of servitization.

Part 2

Competing Through Services

In this second part we explain what it means for a manufacturer to compete through services. We do this in two steps.

In Chapter 3 we focus on the offering itself. We first explain why it can be difficult to understand the concept of servitization, and then explain the process, and define different forms of services. We then focus exclusively on advanced services. We define these and introduce the features that are commonly coupled to these (life-cycles, risks and rewards). We conclude this chapter by consolidating our description of advanced services.

In Chapter 4 we focus on the potential business implications of advanced services. We first explain the difficulties of finding reliable indicators of success and how we have navigated these. We then examine the relationships between services, revenue and profit. In addition, we also examine the broader motives that are shared by manufacturers who are leading providers of advanced services, along with the equivalent motives that are shared by their customers. We conclude this chapter by providing a roadmap of the servitization landscape.

In summary, the picture that these two chapters reveal is:

Servitization process:

- Occurs where a manufacturer develops its capabilities to compete through services.

- These manufacturers are seen as adopting a services-led competitive strategy.

- Some manufacturers follow a service-led strategy by offering a broader portfolio of conventional (base and intermediate) services.

- Other manufacturers largely abandon their design and production capabilities and become pure-services providers.

- Our focus is on those manufacturers that follow a services-led competitive strategy by delivering advanced services.

Advanced services:

- The outcomes for the customer are the capabilities that arise from the use of the manufacturer's products.

- For the manufacturer they represent a significant organizational stretch from production-based competences.

- Advanced services commonly feature extended life-cycles, extended responsibilities (and so risks) and increasingly regular revenue payments.

- Companies who develop these advanced services are commonly setting out to:

  - Target customers' pains (costs) and gains (profits).

  - Grow through business process innovations.

  - Develop long-term relationships that lock out competitors.

  - Develop resilient cash flow and revenue streams.

- These advanced services deliver high value through their potential to:

  - Increase revenue.

  - Increase profits.

  - Smooth revenue streams.

On completing this part of the book, our intention is that the reader understands exactly what is being offered through advanced services and the likely business implications. Armed with this knowledge, our next part explains how organizations are configured to deliver these successfully.

Chapter 3

ELEMENTS OF SERVITIZATION

Servitization is an intriguing concept. As we have just seen, various factors are conducive to services forming the backbone of a manufacturer's competitive advantage. The challenge is to translate this idea into practice.

In 2006, at the start of our research programme, we set out to contrast the world of production to that of one where a manufacturer competes through services by carefully surveying as many manufacturers as possible and reviewing extensive work on servitization in the academic and technical press. We also engaged with Rolls-Royce Civil Aerospace in a significant in-depth study of their power-by-the-hour and TotalCare offerings, along with their journey to develop and sustain these. As a team we studied all aspects of their services design and delivery system, reaching out to their customers and suppliers, and systematically collecting information as we progressed. Ours would prove to be one of the most comprehensive studies undertaken of an industrial product–service system and its associated servitization process.

The differences we saw were not immediately striking. The physical buildings, technologies and products all looked like those we would find in production. The same seemed to be true for the information systems, process guides, organization structures and people. Only the condition monitoring technologies along with their associated technical centres and control rooms seemed to appear out of place. There was no Eureka moment. Our frustrations were compounded by our own mindsets; the core members of our team had been chosen because of their competence and experience in analysing, designing and operating manufacturing plants. Similarly, many of the academic articles we were reading were guiding our thinking into somewhat philosophical debates around the distinctions between products and services. Quite simply what we were being shown was not what we expected to find.

The picture eventually became clear. There are strong distinctions between the world of production and that of a manufacturer competing through services. Yet fully establishing this took a further four years of engaging and studying some of the world's leading manufacturers who were competing in this way. How these organizations thought and talked about services, and how they set about delivering their offerings successfully, all became clear. But this was a challenging journey. *Why did we choose the organizations we did? What forms of services do they offer to their customers? And what are the business benefits they have experienced?* All these questions had to be addressed before we could explore further.

In this and the following chapter we answer these questions. As a precursor, we first explain why it can be difficult at the outset to visualize what it can mean to servitize, and present a roadmap to help navigate this landscape. We then proceed to show how services can be rationalized into three different categories. Our focus then moves specifically to 'advanced' services which are readily associated with servitization. We delve into the distinctive features of these, explore the motivations that have enticed companies to adopt them, and summarize the associated risks and rewards.

3.1 The Challenge of Visualizing What it Can Mean to Servitize

Servitization constitutes a revolution in manufacturing. The motive that has underpinned this whole research programme is to help manufacturers in developed economies to innovate and exploit the opportunities offered by servitization. Throughout, we have kept ourselves grounded by repeatedly visiting and interviewing practitioners from more traditional manufacturers, seeking their opinion about the potential impact of servitization on their organizations.

Time and time again we have been asked by manufacturers to explain this phenomenon, describe what it can look like for them, the services they might offer, and the rewards they can expect. Expectations are high. At the beginning of our programme we would introduce servitization by describing it simply as adding services to products. We would gain traction during conversations by describing individual services such as helpdesks, condition monitoring and maintenance. Finally, we would describe 'pay per use' services such as Rolls-Royce's power-by-the-hour model. We found our responses would be received with great interest initially, and then the enthusiasm would frequently wane.

All too often we would be told that such a model would be too ambitious for most conventional manufacturers, or in some cases irrelevant, and we would then be asked for more 'pragmatic' suggestions. If we responded by giving a conservative suggestion (such as engagement in 'design for manufacture services') we would then be told that this is too simplistic, that it was already being done, or that there was too little value in such services. Dispirited, we came to realize that two factors were undermining our attempts to explain what it means to servitize; language and mindsets.

Complexity arises partly because companies do not share a common 'language' for describing services. There are strong colloquialisms and, to the independent observer, the terms of reference seem fluid and vague. For example, a service offering is sometimes named around a principal 'activity' involved, such as:

- Scheduled maintenance service.

- Repair service.

- Overhaul service.

- Condition monitoring service.

- An oil sampling service.

On other occasions a services offering is referred to as the contractual agreement, such as:

- A risk and revenue sharing contract.

- An availability contract.

- An outcome contract.

- A capability contract.

- A fleet management contract.

Such terminology is ambiguous. There is always a contractual agreement implicit in the purchase of an offering, and every contractual agreement will have an associated set of service activities.

This situation is compounded by managers interchanging the way in which they use the word 'service'. Sometimes it is used as a noun to name an activity (as above), while on other occasions it is used as a verb to describe performance. This can make conversations difficult to follow.

The language and terminology that manufacturers use when referring to services (and hence servitization) clearly has yet to mature – this is reminiscent of how many western manufacturers lost their way with the word quality in the early 1980s. Yet there is a more fundamental issue that is rooted in the mindsets of practitioners.

Many senior managers within manufacturing companies struggle to visualize servitization. This reflects our own experiences at the outset of this research programme. Just as we found for ourselves, the situation is especially complex for people with a strong production heritage. Their worldview or paradigm leads them to expect that services should feature in a manufacturer's strategy in a particular way – somewhat similar to adding additional features to a product. Furthermore, such production people see their organizations as being distinctly different from those which are pure-service providers: banks, hotels, hospitals and call centres. Figure 3.1 illustrates this situation as two polarized positions on a spectrum of knowledge.

People from a traditional manufacturing background are most likely to sit to the left of this spectrum. Their expertise is with

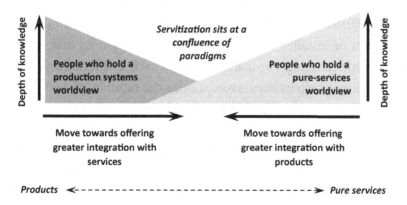

Figure 3.1: *Clashing worldviews of products and services*

production systems and their knowledge of services is limited. The services they understand are those which can be related directly back to production. For instance, an equipment manufacturer might explore carrying out on-site installation and commissioning. They will look for value from each service in isolation, and use this information to judge whether or not to offer that service.

Conversely, people from pure-service organizations will sit at the other extreme. Their expertise is with service systems, and the only production concepts they will understand are those that are easily related to services. As with production people, they will use their own particular terminology and concepts. Rather than talking about 'manufacturing operations', for example, they are likely to refer to service delivery systems and technology-enabled business models.

The topic of servitization sits at the confluence of these two worldviews and borrows ideas from each. An unfortunate consequence is that some people from the production systems world can struggle to envisage ambitious services offerings; by contrast people with a service systems view can struggle to see value in products and technological competences.

Yet this is exactly the position taken by those organizations that are leading through servitization. Rolls-Royce, Caterpillar (and dealers), Alstom and MAN would all associate with this central zone. Xerox helps to illustrate the mindset needed; it no longer quotes figures for population or installed base of printers as this suggests that 'more is better' (which it is not!). Instead, Xerox sees itself as offering a managed print service to help its clients to optimize the number of devices they have and how they are used. This would be an anathema to production people.

As this chapter unfolds it will describe what it means for manufacturers to servitize. As an aid to navigating this and beginning to understand what it means, Figure 3.2 offers an initial roadmap of the servitization landscape.

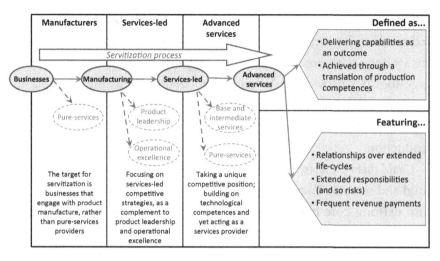

Figure 3.2: *An emergent roadmap of the servitization landscape*

3.2 A Process of Servitization

Generally, servitization is taken as a process where a manufacturer develops its capabilities to compete through services. This is illustrated as the route from left to right in Figure 3.2. Often this conjures an image of a manufacturer adding more and more services to a product platform. *But, is this really what is intended when the concept is discussed and promoted? How does it fit with other ways of competing? And, is it exclusive to manufacturing companies?*

The process suggests a change in the way the business competes. The target business itself needs to be in manufacturing and will servitize by transitioning from just production to acting increasingly as a services provider. The services it comes to offer are not necessarily new; the innovation comes about because it's the manufacturer that is seeking to offer these.

Pure-service providers can set out to offer the same services. They may also extend their technological capabilities to design and engineer replacement products and parts. This is the productization of services and tends to be rare. During our programme we casually discussed this strategy with organizations such as Unipart and Wincanton (both large logistics providers). While not formally dismissing the option, we were left with no doubt; they would require considerable incentives for them to develop their capabilities in product design and production.

Could this be a missed opportunity? Such capabilities are expensive to build and sustain. They are also unlikely to be perceived as fitting well with existing core competences. If they are essential for a particular contract, then partnerships and joint ventures are always a possibility. Yet, just as servitization is now seen as valuable for manufacturers, it might be a little cavalier to dismiss the productization of services.

Pure-services providers are often the principal competitors for manufacturers moving into services. For instance, maintenance on MAN trucks can be carried out by MAN themselves, or the customer – should they have the facilities – or a third party provider. Often, these third parties are small, owner operated, mobile workshops. The point is that the services 'are being carried out'. It's just really a case of who does these currently, and who might be best placed to do so in the future.

Manufacturing businesses themselves have various competitive strategies that they can adopt. Michael Treacy and Fred Wiersema suggest this through their work on value disciplines. They recognize that some market leaders succeed through their product leadership and so invest heavily in product-related innovations. Some focus on operational excellence and succeed through minimizing their costs of production. Still others focus on customer intimacy and build close relationships and bonds with individual companies.

Customer intimacy underpins what we refer to as a services-led competitive strategy. Rather than offering distinctive product performance, or distinctively low product price, the manufacturer leads through distinctive services coupled to their products. This is not to suggest that product performance and operational efficiency are no longer important, they simply don't need to stand out to the same extent as the services offering. Services are never a substitute for a poorly performing product; neither the customer nor the manufacturer can sustain a business in this way.

There are different routes a manufacturer can follow to a services-led competitive strategy (Figure 3.2). One alternative is to build a broad portfolio of relatively conventional services. For instance, they may offer a helpdesk for customers, a repair service, maintenance plans, training, and even factory tours. We refer to these as base and intermediate services and will return to discuss them further in the following section.

A second alternative is for the manufacturer to develop or acquire services that are independent of the products it makes. Such services are offered by organizations like IBM, and can be thought of as macro-servitization. Often these businesses have seen their traditional markets disappear and so are reinventing themselves largely as services-led technology companies by moving into areas such as general consulting and supply chain management. Although technical competences remain important to these companies, they have now removed their focus so far from production that they would no longer refer to themselves as manufacturers.

A third option is for the manufacturer to offer advanced services. For the moment, we will simply take these as services which are closely coupled with products, to such an extent that they are seen as providing customers with a capability rather than just a physical asset. As we will explain shortly, they have a number of distinctive features, and are exactly the services offerings that are associated with the middle ground illustrated in Figure 3.1.

3.3 Defining Base, Intermediate and Advanced Services

Our focus for servitization is on manufacturers that are choosing to compete through a services-led strategy by delivering advanced services. This is the route we illustrate in our roadmap (Figure 3.2). To better understand this route, we now need to delve further into defining different services offerings.

A popular mental image of a manufacturer is that it makes products; material artefacts capable of causing pain should they drop on your foot! Services provided by manufacturers are thought of as an after-sales activity e.g. repair and overhaul. Underpinning this mental image is the notion that products and services are distinctly different and should be treated separately.

Many models within the academic press build on this definition, illustrating how increasing levels of servitization translate to a change in the balance between products and services in the offering to the customer. They inspire a debate that can easily become very philosophical.

Leading adopters of servitization don't think in this way. Rather than the interplay of products and services, they base their distinction on the value proposition to their customers. Caterpillar dealers illustrate this situation well. When referring to their customers they told us that they have:

- Customers who want to *do it themselves*,

- Customers who want us to *do it with them*, and

- Customers who want us to *do it for them*.

These dealers (as part of the extended Caterpillar organization) recognize that some of their customers will only value the provision of equipment, spare parts and consumables. They will then maintain and repair the equipment themselves in their own facilities. Others will carry out some maintenance themselves, such as periodic oil and filter changes, but engage the dealer should repair or overhaul be needed. Others will simply want to operate the equipment and have the dealer take care of everything else.

Each type of customer achieves particular outcomes from their relationship with the Caterpillar dealer. At the simplest level, the outcome is that the customer gains access to the equipment. We refer to this type of service offering as 'base services'. The outcome at the second level, or from 'intermediate services', is a reassurance that the equipment is maintained appropriately. The outcome at the third level is, however, more complex.

With these 'advanced services' the emphasis moves away from the equipment itself and focuses more on the consequence of its performance. The outcome for the customer is now the capability delivered through the performance of the product. Hence, leading adopters of servitization will frequently refer to engaging the customer in a relationship that has closer associations with strategic repositioning and business process outsourcing than to sales of products and services. The distinctions between these types of services are captured in Table 3.1.

Moving from offering base, through intermediate, to advanced services requires a transfer of 'activities' that were once internal to the customer. In other words, the manufacturer has to stretch its range of activities to take an increasingly large slice of its customers' operations. Picturing these activities is an important step in understanding the services being offered.

It is relatively simple to envisage how a base service, such as providing spare parts, can appear as an offering to a customer. Similarly intermediate services, such as maintenance and repair, conjure an image of a workshop with technicians working on equipment. Yet a

Table 3.1 Categorization of product–services offered by a manufacturer

Type	Defined by	Organizational stretch	Examples of services offered
Base services	An outcome focused on product provision	Based on an execution of production competence (i.e. we know how to build it)	Product/equipment provision, spare part provision, warranty
Intermediate services	An outcome focused on maintenance of product condition	Based on exploitation of production competences to also maintain the condition of products (i.e. because we know how to build it we know how to repair it)	Scheduled maintenance, technical helpdesk, repair, overhaul, delivery to site, installation, operator training, operator certification, condition monitoring, in-field service
Advanced services	An outcome focused on capability delivered through performance of the product	Based on translation of production competences to also manage the product's performance (i.e. because we know how to build it we know how to keep it operational)	Customer support agreement, risk and reward sharing contract, revenue-through-use contract, rental agreement

picture of the activities associated with advanced services is still some-what elusive. *What exactly are the activities associated with advanced services?*

Unfortunately the common practice is to refer to advanced services as 'contracts' rather than the activities on which they are based. Part of the reason for this is that manufacturers bring a complex and extended range of activities together to create an advanced services offering. Some of these are very specific to advanced services.

Advanced services, for instance, demand specific programme man-agement activities. These are very much the glue that holds such contracts together. We mentioned at the beginning of this chapter how, in our initial study of Rolls-Royce, the operations room/control centre had readily stood out. The function of these centres typically includes programme management. Closely coupled to this are plan-ning activities; scheduling times and locations for asset maintenance, recording interventions, logging safety checks, managing resources, and controlling stock.

Advanced services also bring together a wide range of existing services, occasionally referred to as bundling or embedding. Again, it can be difficult to fully appreciate the range of services being offered. To illustrate, take the example of a car being sent into a garage for an engine repair; the repair (or service activity) is seen as the process of stripping down the engine and replacing the faulty or worn compo-nent. Look more closely, however, and you will see that the word 'repair' is somewhat of a simplification. Other activities, which are taken for granted, are embedded in the process; a mechanic might first be engaged to diagnose and locate the faulty component, an admin-istrator might schedule the appointment, spare parts might be ordered, a helpdesk might be contacted, and so on. Yet the general approach is to bundle these under the umbrella term of 'repair'.

This is exactly the situation with advanced services. Advanced services are constructed on a platform of intermediate services, which

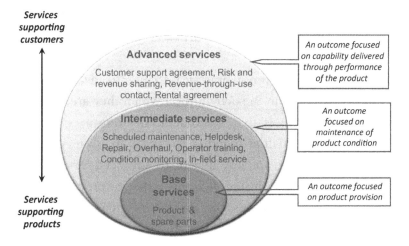

Services
supporting
customers

Advanced services

Customer support agreement, Risk and
revenue sharing, Revenue-through-use
contact, Rental agreement

*An outcome focused
on capability delivered
through performance
of the product*

Intermediate services

Scheduled maintenance, Helpdesk,
Repair, Overhaul, Operator training,
Condition monitoring, In-field service

*An outcome
focused on
maintenance of
product condition*

**Base
services**

Product &
spare parts

*An outcome focused
on product provision*

Services
supporting
products

Figure 3.3: *Services radar diagram illustrating the types of services a manufacturer can offer*

are themselves built on base services. These services can be thought of as building on each other to deliver different outcomes for customers (Table 3.1). This process is illustrated in Figure 3.3. Here, the desired outcome extends from simply 'providing a product' through to 'providing a capability'. Occasionally this is expressed as a transition from 'services supporting products' to 'services supporting customers'.

Advanced services are appealing because they deliver a capability as an outcome. This alone can be appealing for the customer as, for example, it removes the need for product ownership. However, this only partially explains their appeal. In practice, leading adopters of servitization have also coupled particular features to such services. Although these are not in themselves unusual, the resulting offering has distinctive characteristics. We will now explore these further.

3.4 Features Commonly Coupled to Advanced Services

Advanced services focus on delivering capabilities and cause the manufacturer to stretch its activities well beyond production. It's relatively easy to envisage a mechanism whereby the footprint of the customer and manufacturer changes to reflect such services; activities which were once undertaken by the former being carried out by the latter. It's also easy to imagine that all the activities in which the manufacturer now engages are not immediately apparent to the observer. *But is this the complete picture? What other characteristics occur to distinguish between different forms of advanced services?*

Our description of advanced services only goes part way to describing those being offered in practice. A focus on delivering a capability as an outcome is foundational to defining such services. However, manufacturers add other features to the services agreement. For instance, they may flex the process of revenue generations such that the service is paid for as it is consumed; they may adjust the balance of risk that they take in assuring the outcome of the service; and they may agree to deliver such services over an extended life-cycle.

None of these features are themselves unique to advanced services. They may all be applied, in some form, to base and intermediate services. Yet it is popular practice for these to be coupled as additional features to create a sophisticated offering to customers. We will now explore each of these further.

Advanced services usually feature an extended life-cycle

So far we have simply examined the activities involved in the execution of a services offering as these are most readily apparent. But this is just one part of the offering. With advanced services, manufacturers tend to look closely at the extended lifecycle, the activities within this and perhaps most critically how this can be sustained. Furthermore, these life-cycles are almost always lengthy and in some cases stretch over decades.

Although initially transparent to the observer, the life-cycle of advanced services falls into three phases:

1. Generation (or regeneration); service activities carried out to win and sustain a services contract.
2. Deployment; which includes activities carried out to set up and to commission the services offering.
3. Execution; which includes activities carried out in the delivery of the services offering.

Activities associated with *generation* of the contract, such as application consulting, demonstrations and even facility tours are often less apparent because they are management tasks rather than something that happens in a workshop. Yet, as we have seen time and time again during our study, they are extensive and always required.

Such services may also form a bridge between completing one contract and winning another, for instance when there is an agreement to buy back or take on existing equipment from a customer. Those activities associated with *deployment* bridge the generation and execution phases. They include the delivery of equipment, testing and training.

The life-cycle of advanced services contracts is typically very long. Five and ten years are quite common. A contract on a MAN truck may be for five years; a Rolls-Royce TotalCare contract will typically run for ten years; while an Alstom Train Life Services contract may extend beyond 20 years.

Intriguingly some manufacturers will use the term 'through-life' when referring to this life-cycle. They will recognize the three phases but underpinning this is an assumption that these are still related to a particular product sale. The notion of advanced services should, really, surpass this product association. Xerox, for example, fully embraces the notion of delivering a capability as an outcome. They will take on a contract where the customer already has an installed base of a competitor's products, support this equipment, maintain its performance and eventually replace it with their own products.

Advanced services usually feature extended responsibilities, risks and penalties

Risk share refers to the balance of responsibility between the manufacturer and the customer. At one extreme the customer can assume the majority of the risk for equipment functionality, with the manufacturer only offering initial guarantees and warranties. This is usually the case with base and intermediate services.

With advanced services, however, manufacturers tend to take on much greater levels of responsibility. Not only do they focus on outcomes from the performance of their product, but they also take responsibility for these being fulfilled.

With Alstom Train Life Services, for example, this responsibility is defined against the performance, availability and reliability of trains. Performance is concerned with the extent to which the full capability of equipment is delivered. Availability is assessed as the extent of time that a train is available for use, as a proportion of the scheduled availability within an agreed period. Reliability is assessed as a measure of frequency of unpredicted failures. Alstom is assessed against these measures. Should they fail to meet agreed targets, then they are responsible for any corrective action. Furthermore, they incur financial penalties from the customer for any disruption caused while this takes place.

This balance of responsibility and risk does vary across advanced services contracts. A Caterpillar dealership 'Risk and Reward' sharing contract is less arduous than the Alstom example. Here, at the outset of a contract an agreement is made with the customer over equipment availability and the cost to fulfil this. Should the cost of fulfilling this be exceeded, then the Caterpillar dealer will have only half of its costs paid. Alternatively, if the actual costs are lower than those expected, then the Caterpillar dealer is partially compensated for its lost revenue.

So distinctive are these features of responsibility and risk that, on occasion, advanced services contracts are simply viewed in these terms. Rather than focusing on the 'outcome' for a customer, some practitioners take the view that the manufacturer is engaging in increasing levels of risk management. This necessitates a macro-view to be taken of risks, and can follow a rather product-centric view of the services offering.

Advanced services usually feature regular revenue payments

The economic model refers to the timing and process through which funds are transferred. At the outset of our study the economic model of advanced services was somewhat of a mystery. Some academic papers, for instance, led us to believe that 'Rolls-Royce no longer sold engines'. Instead they leased them on a power-by-the-hour basis. *Is this true? If so, how can they afford to do this?* Slowly through our study we unpicked the situation that is common to many advanced services.

Part of the confusion arises because advanced services tend to be highly tailored to individual customers in particular industries. We soon realized that we could not expect to see an aerospace 'power-by-the-hour' contract precisely replicated in the machine tool industry. Slowly the picture cleared. We came to appreciate that when describing the revenue flow, much depends on whether you feature as the customer or the manufacturer, and whether or not you are dealing with capital acquisitions. It also became clear that frequently a financial partner would be involved.

To illustrate, the economic model with 'power-by-the hour' is partially similar to a car leasing scheme. The manufacturer provides the car, but the financial partner provides the resources for the customer to make the purchase. In return the customer enters into an agreement to make regular payments. The bulk of this fee is paid to the financial partner for capital repayment plus interest. However, some portion may go directly to the manufacturer as part of an ongoing maintenance plan.

A similar process of frequent revenue payments is usually associated with advanced services. However, questions are often raised over 'who owns *the equipment/product/asset with advanced services?*' Rarely is it the customer (end user); in this sense those articles in the academic press were accurate. The customer typically makes a regular (e.g. monthly) payment reflecting the lease arrangements and any associated services package. But, rarely is it the manufacturer either, most frequently the financial partner becomes the legal owner of the asset.

This situation was illustrated to the team during visits to the Aircraft Maintenance and Repair depot for Virgin at Heathrow airport. After a guided tour of the facility, we were then shown a gas turbine that was in the process of undergoing a scheduled service check. On the side of the engine a plaque clearly stated that the engine was owned by a financial partner and under mortgage to Virgin Atlantic. A similar plaque was positioned behind the pilot's seat and referred to the whole aircraft.

A final point on this issue, which again causes confusion, is that many of the larger manufacturers have their own financial organizations. In some instances these will be the financial partners, on others an independent organization can be involved. In this sense, the broader

Rolls-Royce organization really can lease engines on a 'power-by-the-hour' basis.

The economic model associated with advanced services is also particular around penalties and usage. Penalties are incorporated into the process in two ways. If the manufacturer's product fails to perform as expected then the customer can draw back payments. Likewise, if the customer fails to use the product as agreed then the manufacturer can receive compensation.

Recalling for the moment the risk and reward sharing contract mentioned above, in the situation where the maintenance costs exceed the agreed fee, then generally they are shared between the manufacturer and customer on a 50/50 split. Should the actual costs be less than expected, then the manufacturer can be partially compensated with a share in the saving.

Advanced services contracts will typically stipulate levels of asset usage. There may be a minimum level agreed – such that the manufacturer will receive a base fee each month – and also a maximum level that should not be exceeded. For example, a Caterpillar quarry truck may be contracted to be available 20 hours each day. Should this be exceeded, the customer is charged a premium.

Such agreements on usage also cover how equipment is used. For instance, an aircraft might be covered for particular routes. This reflects the extra loads placed on an engine during landings and take-offs each day. Should the customer change the route, maybe moving from long haul to regional travel, then premiums might be charged by the manufacturer.

Table 3.2 summarizes this economic model. As a consequence of this economic model advanced services are quite different to base and intermediate. In some instances this is quite straightforward, such as when spare parts are paid for by the customer at the point of collection, or when repairs are made on the basis of time and materials consumed and interim payments are made by the customer.

Table 3.2 Generalized economic model for advanced services

Manufacturer		Financial partner		Customer	
Provides	*Receives*	*Provides*	*Receives*	*Provides*	*Receives*
Product/ equipment	Lump payment	Lump payment	Periodic payment for asset	Periodic payment for asset	Product/ equipment
Maintenance and management services	Periodic payment for services			Periodic payment for services	Maintenance and management services
	Minus penalties for failure to perform			Minus penalties for failure to perform	
	And/or compensation for poor utilization			And/or compensation for poor utilization	

3.5 A Summary of Advanced Services

We began this chapter by explaining that the opportunities presented by servitization can be difficult to visualize for people with a strong background in production. As an aid to navigating this topic we presented a roadmap of the servitization landscape (Figure 3.2). The chapter has followed this, defining servitization, and introducing advanced services and their distinctive features.

The following chapter will complete this journey by summarizing the motives that underpin the adoption of these services and how these then deliver high value. At this interlude, it is helpful to summarize the form that advanced services take.

Figure 3.4 illustrates that base services are at the core of any offering from a manufacturing enterprise. These are concerned with the

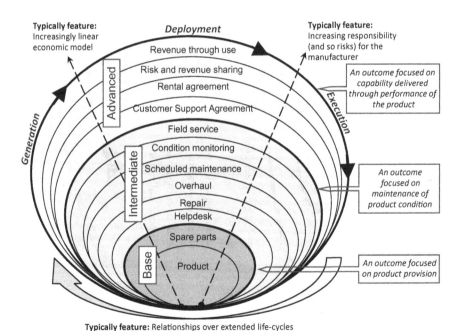

Figure 3.4: *Illustrating the characteristics of advanced services with examples*

initial provision of products (e.g. excavator or machine tool) and associated spare parts.

If the manufacturer then extends into intermediate services, such as repair and overhaul, there is implicitly a greater involvement in ensuring the state and condition of equipment. For example, operator training ensures that equipment is used as intended, scheduled maintenance ensures that oil changes take place as specified, and condition monitoring such as oil sampling helps to highlight any unforeseen deterioration in equipment condition.

These intermediate services embed many base services to focus on the maintenance of product condition. For example, efficient spare parts provision can help to ensure rapid repairs. However, advanced services subsume both base and intermediate services. The outcome they provide is the capability that is delivered through the product's use rather than simply its condition. In practice, manufacturers also combine these with agreements for longer contract life-cycles, increased responsibilities, and more stable revenue flows.

Our illustration has set out to isolate the features of typical advanced services offerings. They are the key elements of the proposition to the customer. Delivery of these services requires the manufacturer to adopt specific practices and technologies. We will explore these shortly, but before doing so we will first examine the motives and benefits that help to explain the appeal of advanced services.

Chapter 4

Servitization is catching the western world's attention because of the successes of companies such as Rolls-Royce. In 2006, when our programme of research commenced, Rolls-Royce earned over 54% of its revenue from services. Indeed, services have made a significant contribution to their income and profitability for the past decade.

Our subsequent study of Rolls-Royce helped us to appreciate that their revenues come from a mix of base, intermediate and advanced services. Rolls Royce will, for example, provide spare parts, undertake to repair engines, and offer 'power-by-the-hour' contracts. The generation of revenue from such a mix of services transpired to be apparent in all the companies we would later come to study.

Our initial questions were clear. *How do different types of services contribute to revenue generation, and also how do they contribute to profitability?* But we also recognized that such financial results, while alone being powerful motivators, would only partially explain the value of services to manufacturers.

There would be other reasons why manufacturers favoured a servitization strategy. Similarly, there would be a complementary set of reasons that explain why customers were receptive to such a strategy. Our interest focused explicitly on advanced service. We therefore set out to question: *what are the principal strategic motives that explain why manufacturers and their customers are adopting advanced services?*

This chapter describes how we went about investigating this aspect of servitization and presents what we now know.

4.1 Setting Out to Explore Financial Performance

Throughout the research programme we could envisage the principal question that senior executives would ask: *will we make any money through servitization?* The strategies and subsequently the successes of many firms would be influenced by what we reported. Our challenge was therefore to provide reliable answers.

Earlier studies of Just-in-Time and Lean production suggested possible approaches to our work. Seminal books, such as *The Machine that Changed the World*, were based on an extensive international survey of the automotive industry, identification of the better performers, and then a systematic investigation of an outstanding business. In this instance Toyota. There are clear parallels between the phenomena of servitization and Lean production. *Could we follow a similar process, could we apply survey techniques, and could we find our equivalent of Toyota?*

Our first step was to carry out a small-scale survey. Through late 2008 and early 2009 we surveyed manufacturers in the UK who we might expect to offer advanced services. The results were promising. We saw that only one in four UK companies was building its services portfolio, but almost all of these reported that the profitability of services was generally higher than (or at the worst equivalent to) that of new product sales. Their reasons for providing such services were principally:

1. Improving ability to respond to customer needs.
2. Increasing differentiation from competitors.

3. Increasing customer loyalty.
4. Building new revenue streams.
5. Setting barriers to competitors.

Unfortunately our delight in uncovering these findings was short-lived. When we took a closer look at our data some issues regarding consistency opened up and we became uncomfortable with the reliability of the answers we had been given. Significant variations and omissions were apparent, especially with regards to financial results. So, in an attempt to uncover what was causing these, we visited a selection of the surveyed companies to discuss their written responses. Three factors appeared that subsequently convinced us that we would have to drastically change the way we studied servitization; these were:

1. *Extent of success was not known:* Managers often didn't know how well services were benefiting their organization financially. Indeed some respondents were so interested in this issue that they had circulated our questionnaire within their own organizations, in an attempt to find out these results for themselves.

2. *Financial reporting conventions differ:* The conventions and assumptions underpinning financial reports can vary from one organization to another. The manufacturer can choose different mechanisms to apportion costs and revenue within their organization. It is quite possible for direct profit on more advanced services to appear low, but for overall profits of the organization to be improved. This can occur where there are favourable taxation regulations on the subsequent sale of used (ex-service contract) equipment, or where the spare parts used by an internal service organization are charged at full retail price.

3. *Services-led strategies differ:* Manufacturers build their services portfolios in different ways. Some simply deliver a greater volume of

base and intermediate services. Others change the types of services on offer and move into advanced services. The latter types of services were the focus for our study, but all too often they can become confused with the former.

Surveying organizations was simply not sufficient. We needed to adopt a research method that would enable us to look more deeply, especially into the financial results arising through servitization. We were looking for information that was representative of an organization's performance, unaffected by differing financial conventions, and specifically targeting advanced services.

We changed our research method. The choice we made was to apply 'Delphi' techniques to a broad cross-section of manufacturers. Case by case we first gathered information on types of services offered, questioned managers on their perceptions of the impact on financial success, aggregated the results, and iteratively returned to those managers until we gained a consistent answer that we could explain.

This approach served our purpose. Although we would be unable to make broader predictions about, for example, the value of servitization to an economy, we would be able to confidently gauge how competing through the provision of advanced services might impact an individual manufacturing organization. We would come to understand the financial results and broader benefits arising from these. This we can now share.

4.2 Services, Revenues and Profitability

By studying a broad cross-cross section of manufacturers a picture emerged of the relationship between the types of services provided to a customer, the revenue earned, and the resulting profit. Taking the organization as a whole (grouping both production and service activities) then in general the relationships appear as:

1. Revenue earned by a manufacturer from a customer increases with a move from base to advanced services.
2. Overall profits earned by the manufacturer also increase with a move from base to advanced services, though not in proportion to revenue.

Our focus was exclusively on the servitization route shown in Figure 3.2, where a manufacturer progresses from delivering base services (e.g. products and spare parts), through intermediate services (e.g. maintenance, condition monitoring, field services), and then to advanced services (e.g. power-by-the-hour), rather than simply increasing its portfolio of base and intermediate services.

This process of increasing services provision naturally brings with it a growth in revenue generation as the manufacturer undertakes more work for its customer. To put it simply, the manufacturer is gaining a larger and larger slice of its customer's business. Figure 4.1 illustrates this relationship. This comes about if the manufacturer is successful in taking over, and selling back to the customer, services that the customer has traditionally performed itself.

There appears, however, to be a natural limit to the extent of revenue growth. This is the point where the offer of further services

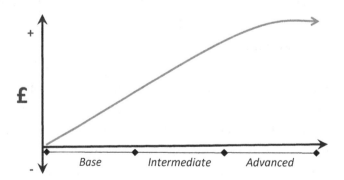

Figure 4.1: *Total revenue earned by a manufacturer from a customer for different types of services*

by the manufacturer will not automatically result in greater revenues from the customer. This point will vary from customer to customer, market to market, and perhaps industry to industry. Some will see much greater benefits in advanced services than others, and want to adopt more comprehensive offerings. Others will be more cautious.

The point at which a customer's appetite slows reflects their perception of the benefits they will receive. Should the manufacturer's services be perceived as beginning to encroach on the core activities of the customer then their value will be reduced. Indeed they may be seen as a threat by the customer.

This situation appeared across the companies we studied. For example, Alstom would not provide drivers for Virgin's trains; MAN would not employ drivers for Hoyer's trucks; and Caterpillar dealers would not remove ore from mines and quarries. Each of these companies recognized a limit to what their customers valued. When we enquired further, the situation was succinctly captured by a vice president of services within a Caterpillar dealership, who summed up the situation as '. . . *this would put us in competition with our customers'*.

An equilibrium therefore appears between the manufacturer and its customers; a balance is reached where the competences of the manufacturer are thoroughly exploited and yet those of the customer remain distinctive. Revenue received by the manufacturer will plateau (see Figure 4.1), and this point will naturally change overtime.

There is, however, a more treacherous scenario. As we mentioned in the previous chapter, manufacturers frequently couple advanced services with agreements over risk adoption. In some instances they will take extensive responsibilities for the performance of their products. Should they fail to meet these, then the customer will be financially compensated through penalty agreements. In effect, revenue payments made by the customer are returned, and overall the manufacturer actually receives less revenue. While such a situation will affect revenue, it will have a more immediate and dramatic impact on profitability.

Much is said in the wider management literature about profits from services. In Table 2.2 (Chapter 2), for example, we cited cases where profits from services were greater than those from product sales. In practice the situation is complex, with distinctions between base, intermediate and advanced services rarely being clear.

In general the total value of profits increases although margins reduce. Researchers often refer to this as the 'service paradox' where revenues may increase but profits actually decrease with greater servitization. Profit levels can be maintained, but only if the manufacturer prices service contracts appropriately, and then manages the costs and risks over the lifetime of the contract. The delivery of advanced services impacts profit margins in a number of ways, including:

1. *Economies of scale are eroded:* The increased organizational stretch demanded of the manufacturer can adversely affect the internal efficiency and effectiveness. As we discuss in detail in later chapters, advanced services by their nature move the manufacturer away from centralized production facilities. As they do so economies of scale are reduced and so the cost of delivery increases.

2. Additional resources (people and skills, technology) may be needed to deliver against the 'promise' to the customer and this will increase overhead.

3. *Advanced services contracts are easily oversold:* Such contracts represent very significant business opportunities which are so appealing that manufacturers are tempted to be very generous when designing their offering. Should they be too ambitious, or fail to understand their own costs thoroughly, they can significantly compromise their own profit margins.

4. *Advanced services contracts often include penalty clauses:* Just as we mentioned above for revenue, if a contract includes penalty payments for poor performance, then any failure to deliver will directly impact profitability.

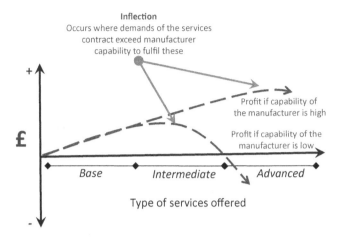

Figure 4.2: *Total profit earned by a manufacturer from a customer for different types of services*

These factors can interplay in such a way that there is a significant variance in the profit arising from advanced services contracts. Figure 4.2 illustrates this situation.

These relationships with both revenue and profit help to explain the appeal, at least financially, of advanced services for customers. More traditionally services business models were such that, should a product or asset fail and require substantial repairs, then the revenue recouped by the manufacturer was proportional to the time and materials taken to carry out such repairs. The customer was wholly responsible for these costs once the product or asset was outside of any warranty period. This situation is illustrated in Figure 4.3a.

The reverse is true of advanced services. The longer a product or asset is out of operation, the greater are the costs accrued by the manufacturer (Figure 4.3b). The extent of these costs does vary for different forms of advanced service. In some instances, the penalties can be so severe that the manufacturer is likely to hold products or assets in reserve at the customer's facilities.

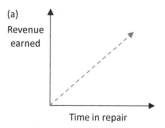

Figure 4.3a: *For a conventional repair contract revenue earned is proportional to time taken in repair*

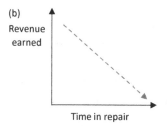

Figure 4.3b: *For an advanced services contract revenue earned is inversely proportional to time taken in repair*

Frequently the manufacturer takes on much greater responsibilities than they would for base and intermediate services. In doing so, they run a risk that they don't have their own capabilities in place to fulfil these. Hence, it is very important that a manufacturer understands the practices and technologies that are needed to support advanced services contracts. We therefore delve into these in the following chapters of this book.

4.3 Motivations of Manufacturers Providing Advanced Services

Henry Ford saw his business objective as service (value to the customer) and profit came naturally as a result. During our research programme we saw that the senior executives of leading manufacturers thought in a similar way. They had clear reasons for adopting advanced services which ultimately led to their businesses being more financially successful.

We set out to understand these reasons by posing the question: *Why are these manufacturers adopting a servitization strategy?* Here, we were careful to avoid discussing the particular incidents or circumstances that had set organizations on this path. Although interesting, we were eager to focus on those motives that were fostering growth and sustainability of a strategy.

What we found is that there are four principal factors that leading adopters of servitization have in common. Their strategies focus on:

1. Helping their customers to be successful; addressing their business 'pains' (costs) and helping them to 'gain' (profits).
2. Growing their businesses through opening up new revenue streams with existing customers through process innovations.
3. Developing long-term business relationships that lock out competitors.
4. Developing resilient cash flow and revenue streams.

Putting these in context is helpful here in appreciating the different factors. Often manufacturers' emphasis is on product sales, and they sell services in much the same way as they sell products. Most compete through product innovations, many have transactional relationships with their customers, and their exposure to competitors with lower-cost bases is high. With these thoughts in mind, we will now explore more fully each motivation in the list above.

Helping customers to be successful; addressing their business pains and helping them to gain

This motivation was universal across our case companies but manifested itself in differing ways. The surrogate for 'pains' is usually costs, and for 'gains' profit. This offensive strategy was common to the companies we studied, their organizational goals and their approaches to achieving these.

An encounter at a Caterpillar dealer conference illustrated this situation well. We were visiting the vice president of services at a successful dealership in Texas. They had been with the company over 30 years and was reciting experiences of their first dealer conference. The V.P. described being introduced, soon after arrival, to the principal (owner) of one of the most successful dealers in the USA.

The conversation naturally moved onto *'so what's your job in the business?'* Our senior manager somewhat innocently replied he was a service manager. *'No'*, replied the principal. *'I asked what is your job?'* *'Oh, I sell parts and services'*, replied the manager. To which the principal's response was *'no, your job is to help your customer to become as rich as possible!'*

Initially taken aback by the forcefulness of this repost, the senior manager subsequently came to appreciate that the principal was telling him to look beyond simply selling products and/or services. Instead, his focus should be on the outcome these provided for the customer. This manager subsequently adopted this 'mantra' throughout his career.

Such a motive is common. Other Caterpillar dealers describe their actions as embedding themselves into the customer's organization far enough to help that customer realize the full value of the product and support offerings. Xerox similarly describe itself as helping its customers to become more successful in their markets – and *not* simply trying to sell more and more volume or more equipment.

This same motive was seen also with MAN. Understanding that fuel represents around 50% of the operating cost of a truck, MAN designed their 'Trucknology' service offering to potentially reduce fuel consumption by up to 10% (this equates to £5000 per vehicle per year – a huge benefit when large fleet operators will run as many as

1000 trucks). As a consequence, MAN have identified that many of their customers only fully utilize trucks some 23% of the time; they see their challenge as helping to significantly increase this figure.

This mindset is key to the services-led approach – focusing on selling neither products nor services, but instead helping customers to be more successful in their own businesses. Debates about the relative importance of products and services are artificial. Customer success is dependent on an integration of both. When a customer is success-ful, this generates both new services business and an opportunity to sell more equipment; the greater the contribution to customer success, the greater the value to the customer, and the greater the opportunity for revenue generation. These are pre-emptive growth-driven strate-gies, and we have set out to capture this mechanism in the influence diagram shown in Figure 4.4.

Growing business through opening up new revenue streams with existing customers through process innovations

Alstom's strategy for Virgin Trains is a prime example of this. When Virgin acquired the franchise to operate trains on the West Coast

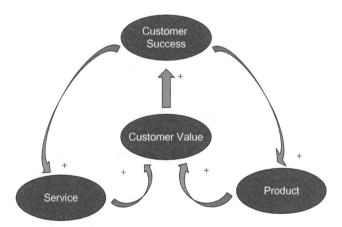

Figure 4.4: *Interdependencies of both services and equipment in revenue generation*

Mainline in the UK they focused their business on promoting rail transport, selling and collecting fares, and driving trains. They did not get involved with train manufacture or services supporting the use of the train (spares, repair and maintenance).

Alstom were innovative with their business process. They created an organization called Train Life Services, and offered the Pendolino trains to Virgin on availability contracts. Had the train manufacturer Alstom only focused on building and selling trains and providing spare parts, it is difficult to see how they would have attracted Virgin's business. Similar incidences have occurred in other industries. Rolls-Royce were motivated to develop their power-by-the-hour/TotalCare offerings, by American Airlines

In some instances these advanced services might necessitate that the manufacturer assumes responsibility for a portfolio of equipment including multi-vendor products. Xerox, for example, will take on contracts where customers already have a large installed base of multi-vendor printing/copying machines (e.g. H-P, Fujitsu, Canon). Caterpillar dealers will take similar contracts covering John Deere, Case and Volvo equipment. Once the contract is operational, this equipment will be slowly replaced by the manufacturers' own products.

In other instances, by providing services the manufacturer is engaging customers that it would have otherwise failed to reach. An example from this study was a landfill operation carried out by the local city council at a site in California that was in close proximity to a military installation. The council was constrained from outsourcing the operation to a non-government agency, and yet were obliged to minimize their ownership of capital assets. Consequentially, they entered into a range of revenue-through-use contracts with the Caterpillar dealership in the region. These were described by the associated vice president of services as *'we provide everything except three things; the operators, the fuel, and the abuse of the equipment'*.

This last point was a light-hearted reference to the responsibility for equipment damage through misuse attributed to the customer. So precise were these contracts that they required the Caterpillar dealer to start up the machinery in the morning and hand it over to the operator at the start of his or her shift, and then be available to receive the equipment back at the end of the shift to shut it down. Similar incentives arose when the taxation conventions in the region meant that used (ex-contract) equipment was subject to lower sales taxes than new.

Developing long-term business relationships that lock out competitors

If the first two motivations are offensive then this is defensive. The spares and repairs market, for western manufacturers, is constantly being challenged. Producers from lower cost economies can produce cheap pattern parts, perhaps without as much concern for their reputation and standards at the original manufacturer. Moreover, small, independent contractors can offer maintenance and small-scale repair services using such non-OEM manufactured parts. This situation impacts the product manufacturer in a number of ways, in particular it:

- Reduces revenue for replacement parts and service sales.

- Exposes the manufacturer's product to inferior parts and services, potentially impacting product reliability and performance, which can in turn harm the product's reputation.

- Potentially provides a foothold for the competition from which to grow and expand its product and/or service offerings.

The provision of advanced services enables the original equipment manufacturer to close down this avenue. One Caterpillar dealer commented *'It's about locking up the orchard.'* He was describing how having the product in the field was simply like having apple trees in an orchard. The revenue from service parts and sales, the 'fruit', and advanced services ensured that it was picked by the dealer as opposed to being stolen by competitors gaining entry into the 'orchard'.

Intensifying the relationship with customers facilitates additional product sales and services opportunities. For example, rather than simply selling spare parts for an excavator from a central depot, a Caterpillar dealer providing advanced services will go into the field and deal directly with the equipment operator. In this way, grassroots relationships are developed, and more detailed knowledge of the application is formed, both of which mean that the manufacturing enterprise is in a stronger position to sell on services and products through a better understanding of the customer's business requirements.

Developing resilient cash flow and revenue streams

Advanced services can improve and smooth revenue streams. The recent recession illustrates this opportunity. Caterpillar dealers, for example, report occasions where equipment sales have declined by as much as 90% but equipment rental was only down by 25% in the same period.

This often occurs because during an economic downturn a customer might hold back on investing in new products, but may be prepared to lease equipment or extend the lifetime of existing products by entering into advanced services contracts. Therefore, reduced product sales revenue generation is offset by a growth in revenues from the provision of advanced services for products in the installed base. Hence over time the overall revenue stream is smoother.

By contrast, during periods of heightened product demand, advanced services contracts can again be used to smooth revenue flow. Quite often the manufacturer can influence the particular item of equipment being deployed on a contract. In this case, the contract will specify the type and number of machines that are to be available, but not necessarily which machine on a particular day. The manufacturer can therefore choose to replace a machine earlier than planned should they have a lull in demand, or conversely delay its replacement should demand for new product sales increase.

In this sense, the advanced services contract becomes an equipment reservoir for the manufacturer. Over this time the revenue to the manufacturing enterprise will be relatively reliable and predictable, and protected from competitors who offer lower cost parts and services.

4.4 Motivations of Customers Adopting Advanced Services

Manufacturers might have strong strategic business reasons for developing their advanced services offerings but, for them to gain adoption in the market, these must appeal to customers. During the study we set out to understand these reasons by posing the question: *Why are customers adopting advanced services?*

Again, we were careful to avoid discussing the particular incidents or circumstances that had initially led organizations onto a servitization path, choosing instead to focus on more enduring motives. Five factors stood out:

1. Reducing operating costs and improving product/asset performance.
2. Enabling management teams to focus energies on core business activities.
3. Transferring fixed costs into variable costs that reflect revenue generation.

4. Improving financial visibility.
5. Reducing risks and barriers of acquiring and operating new technologies.

In themselves these reasons do not appear to be exceptional. However, advanced services can fulfil these in particular ways. We will now explore these in turn.

Reducing operating costs and improving the product/asset performance

This factor arose time and time again during our discussion with customers of advanced services. While appreciating the motive, we were initially uncertain of the mechanism. *How can advanced services reduce operating costs?*

Initially we expected this to be achieved by better matching of capacity with demand. As we explain below, advanced services contracts such as power-by-the-hour help the customer to better balance their income generation and operating costs. However, customers were not referring to this process in this instance. Operating costs reduce because the manufacturer is best placed to ensure the efficiency and effectiveness of the products and assets they produce. In particular they can:

1. Ensure that the right product/equipment is available for a specific task. The manufacturer is likely to have access to a greater pool of equipment resources; whereas customers who have purchased particular equipment will need to use this for a variety of tasks.
2. Transfer products/equipment between contracts to compensate for fluctuation in demands. The manufacturer will also be able to flex the number of products/resources available to a task.
3. Redesign or modify products/equipment so that they perform better and are easier to maintain. Should a product/equipment fail

in service, the manufacturer has the capability to modify the design to avoid future problems. They can also modify designs so that, for example, access for maintenance is easier.

4. Exploit relationships with suppliers to ensure parts and labour are readily available. Manufacturers are likely to have much stronger relationships with their own suppliers, and so have better leverage than their customers will have.

As a consequence of these factors, manufacturers can drive down the costs of supporting an advanced services contract. These advantages can then be exploited to incentivize customers to adopt such contracts by reducing operating costs for the customer.

These factors are also likely to mean that product/asset performance is improved. Furthermore, when these are coupled with the financial agreements we discussed earlier, the manufacturer has strong incentives to ensure that any product or equipment performs to agreed standards.

Enabling the management team to focus energies on core business activities

Our study found many good examples of this motivation to adopt advanced services in customers of all the companies we studied.

Customers of Caterpillar dealers would, for instance, see their core business activities as ore extraction. They would focus on the acquisition of quarries and mines, understanding the geology of the area, and managing the subsequent excavation and extraction processes. For such customers, maintaining a maintenance facility for quarry trucks, along with the associated people and equipment, was an unnecessary investment of time and money in non-core business activities. The proposition to carry out such activities was a key incentive in adopting advanced services contacts on their quarry trucks.

Similar situations arose between Alstom and Virgin. The competences of Virgin Rail would centre on managing trains and their drivers, selling the tickets and marketing their service to passengers. Virgin Rail was able to leave other activities to Alstom under their 'availability' contract.

Similarly, the 'Trucknology' fleet management offering from MAN UK to logistics giant Hoyer was adopted to enable Hoyer to focus on the delivery of bulk materials (food, gas, mineral fuels, etc.) to its customers while MAN took care of their vehicle fleet, guaranteeing a fixed pence per kilometre cost and vehicle availability based around on-time customer delivery for Hoyer.

Transfer fixed costs into variable costs that reflect revenue generation

On occasions, advanced services may not reduce total operating costs. Under some conditions, such as high levels of utilization, some can be expensive alternatives. For example, a commercial aircraft on a power-by-the-hour contract might, under certain conditions, be more expensive for a customer to operate than one on a more conventional leasing agreement.

Even then, advanced services can hold value for a customer. One advantage is that they frequently reduce fixed costs for the customer. Instead of the customer outlaying funds for initial product/equipment purchase, they may enter into an agreement where they pay regular instalments. These instalments can cover both the asset lease and associated services (see section 3.4).

These payments are often linked to usage. The most illustrative example of this is power-by-the-hour on an aircraft engine. Here, the customer makes regular payments that reflect the number of hours flown. There are maximum and minimum limits to such agreements. If the aircraft is not used, the airline customer will still be responsible for a relatively small fee. If the aircraft is overused, or perhaps used on routes where there are adverse conditions (frequent landings or landings in desert regions), then the airline will be penalized.

During this study we came to appreciate how a large airline operator might have aircraft under a variety of contracts. Some they might own entirely. These will be maintained by the airline's own maintenance people, and are likely to be most heavily scheduled for use. Then there will be other aircraft which are on a long-term lease, but again maintained by the airline's personnel. Conditions of the lease may cause the operator to be more selective on scheduling and routing for these aircraft. The airline may then retain some aircraft on a power-by-the-hour basis. They may not be responsible for the maintenance of these, and they only used to deal with capacity fluctuations in airline travel. When a downturn in demands hits, these are the aircraft that 'sit on the tarmac first'.

Improving financial visibility

Where a customer carries out services, which might otherwise be provided by a manufacturer, they carry these costs within their organization. However, they may not fully appreciate the true costs of providing such services.

Organizations rely on accounting conventions to determine cost. Methods such as 'allocation and absorption costing' and 'marginal costing' are popular. These all use different assumptions, conventions or rules to calculate a cost for carrying out a business activity. Such assumptions restrict the reliability with which costs can be usefully calculated.

When entering into an advanced services contract the customer, in effect, transfers the ownership of cost calculation to the manufacturer. Internal costing systems are no longer needed. Instead the customer has clear visibility of costs for today, and stretching out into the future.

Reducing risks and barriers of acquiring and operating new technologies

Power-by-the-hour is an iconic example of an advanced service, and it is directly associated with Rolls-Royce. Yet the origins are rooted in the practices of the aircraft manufacturer Bristol Siddeley. In the 1960s they launched a new executive jet onto the market. The jet featured a new gas turbine engine named the Viper.

Initially the jet failed to sell in North America. Existing maintenance and repair facilities appeared reluctant to hold spare parts for the Viper engine until significant sales had been made; potential buyers were reluctant to purchase the aircraft until they felt it was supported by maintenance bases. Bristol Siddeley broke this stalemate by creating the power-by-the-hour contract. In effect, using an advanced services contract to gain acceptance of a new technology in the market.

Caterpillar dealers offer a similar example. For some time electrical transmissions have been favoured on large quarry trucks, but have struggled on applications where the haul-road descent was overly long. To overcome this problem Caterpillar developed an alternative mechanical transmission. In order to gain initial acceptance from the market, they coupled the new technology to an advanced services contract. Risk for the customer was significantly reduced and access to improved technology was provided.

For customers, therefore, advanced services offer a low-risk route for new technology adoption. Coupling new technology introduction with an advanced services contract guaranteeing performance, reliability and availability greatly reduces the risk for the customer. The barrier to early adoption of a new product is thereby lowered. In addition, the manufacturer gains an opportunity to introduce a new product into the market, gain feedback on its performance, and subsequently build a new revenue stream.

Barriers around the access to finance can also be reduced. Customers may struggle on their own to raise finance for substantial investment in new products. When partnered with the manufacturer, however, banks can be more willing to lend. Alternatively, the manufacturer themselves may have financial partners already in place that enable advanced services to be adopted by customers.

4.5 A Roadmap of Servitization and Advanced Services

As a corollary to this chapter, and as a precursor to exploring the practices and technologies that are key to delivering advanced services, it is useful to summarize the servitization path we are exploring, the characteristics of advanced services, and why these are of high value for a manufacturer. We have created a roadmap for this in Figure 4.5.

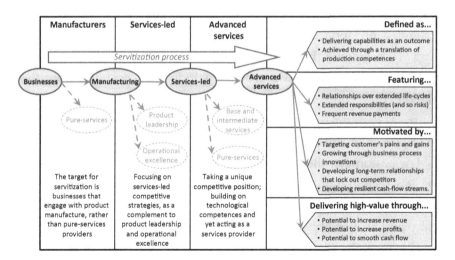

Figure 4.5: *Roadmap of the servitization landscape*

In summary, Figure 4.5 illustrates that servitization is a process where a manufacturer develops its capabilities to compete through services. These manufacturers are seen as adopting a services-led competitive strategy, rather than product leadership or operational excellence. Some manufacturers follow a services-led strategy by offering a broader portfolio of conventional services. Others largely abandon their technological competences and become pure-services providers. Our focus is when the manufacturer acts as a services provider that exploits technological competences to deliver advanced services.

Advanced services provide the customer with capabilities that arise from the use of the manufacturer's products. For the manufacturer they represent a significant organizational stretch from production-based competences. Advanced services also commonly feature extended life-cycles, extended responsibilities (and so risks) and increasingly regular revenue payments.

Those manufacturers that offer advanced services are commonly setting out to grow through business process innovations, and development of long-term relationships that lock out competitors and so develop resilient revenue streams. These advanced services deliver high value to the manufacturer through their potential to increase revenue, increase profits and smooth revenue flow.

There are caveats with servitization that need to be mentioned. To succeed the manufacturer needs to engage with customers that are aligned in their motives, culture and processes. Dangers arise, for instance, with customers that believe that they have to manage the manufacturers' operations (e.g. the extent of labour and stock they have in place) rather than the output from their processes. Where customers are, however, mature, and keen to adopt advanced services, the challenge for manufacturers is to configure their operations to deliver these services offerings effectively and efficiently.

Part 3
Service Delivery System

In this third part we explain the system, technologies and practices that are key to delivering advanced services. We do this in two steps.

In Chapter 5 we establish key terminology and describe the typical structure of a product–service system (PSS). We then focus on the subsystem of such a PSS that sits within the operations of the manufacturer; the service delivery system. We explain the scope of such a system, and the two capabilities that are critical for such a system to perform successfully. In Chapters 6–9, we then examine the technologies and practices that are adopted by those manufacturers that are successfully delivering advanced services.

In summary, these chapters reveal:

Service delivery system:

- Products are delivered by production systems; advanced services are delivered by product–service systems.

- The subset of a product–service system that sits within the operations of a manufacturer is termed the 'service delivery system'.

- The characteristics of service delivery systems are distinctly different to those of production systems.

- Key capabilities of a service delivery system are (1) an ability to respond cost effectively and (2) an ability to improve cost effectiveness.

Technology and practice principles that enable the successful delivery of advanced services:

As a manufacturer moves from production to deploying their products through advanced services they:

- Adopt performance measures that are focused on outcomes aligned to individual customers. These then cascade in various forms throughout the service delivery system, and are complemented by indicators that broadly demonstrate value.

- Develop or adopt facilities, co-located and distributed throughout their customers' operations.

- Extend their responsibilities beyond production, integrating into a wide range of customer activities, through extensive front-office activities aligned around services offered, with design and production capabilities in place to support through life deployment.

- Extend their ICT systems to inform and advance actions of maintenance, repair and use.

- Assign 'front-office' staff, who are skilled in being flexible, relationship builders, service-centric, authentic, technically adept and resilient.

- Extend their processes across a wide range of customer 'touchpoints', fostering strong inter-organizational relationships at these, to manage proactively the condition, use and location of products in the field.

Chapter 5

We discovered that advanced services could positively impact the financial performance of a business but to do so they had to be delivered efficiently and effectively. Our goal was then to understand how those manufacturers leading in servitization went about such delivery. In particular, we wanted to understand the practices and technologies they applied, how these differed to those within production operations, and how they combined as a complete system.

In this chapter we describe the process we followed and the answers we found.

5.1 Searching for Leaders

In principle our task was quite clear. Set out to correlate track records of financial success with differing approaches to the delivery of advanced services, paying particular attention to the practices and technologies that underpin such delivery.

Our aspiration was simple; collect a broad and reliable set of data about the practices of companies. This should capture the revenue and profits for advanced services against a selection of manufacturers, and summarize the technologies and practices they used across their service delivery. For completeness, this data set would also include manufacturers who were failing to deliver together with the strategies they had adopted.

Once again, however, we faced the same issues as when we set out to explore profit and revenue relationships. As we explained in section 4.1, the reliability of financial performance data is undermined by:

- Financial apportionment and reporting conventions differing across organizations.

- Services-led strategies differing in their form.

We looked for ways forward, but as we did so a third issue arose which we had not previously considered. We realized that it was easy to overlook revenues generated by sole distributors and close partners which are, in effect, part of the extended organization of the host, yet are not reported as services by the manufacturer.

So far we had taken the host manufacturer as our 'unit of analysis'. All was well so long as we dealt with organizations that brought together production and service provision under one roof. This approach was limited because it focused our attention on manufacturers with a particular organizational structure.

Our work with Caterpillar helps to highlight the issue we faced. In this organization services are delivered in close collaboration with autonomous dealerships. Only by working across both Caterpillar and their dealers could we gain a reliable and comprehensive insight into their practices and technologies.

Eventually we decided to proceed using a multi-layered filtering process. We would choose those manufacturers that had a history of delivering advanced services; demonstrated sustained financial success; were well respected within the practitioner and research community; and had demonstrable evidence of innovation in their products and processes. Our indicators would include financial performance, citation, patents registered and general reputation within the business community.

We would also be mindful of the extended supply chain of these organizations. To achieve this we would draw into this study the customer, partners and suppliers of the targeted manufacturers. Across all these organizations, we would look in depth at how they went about delivering their advanced service.

This process drove our study towards five organizations: Rolls-Royce, Caterpillar (and dealers), Xerox, MAN and Alstom. These we engaged as core collaborators. In each of these we would come to conduct multiple case studies across their extended supply chain, carrying out in-depth interviews with staff ranging from vice presidents through to field service engineers and operatives, and collecting a broad data set about performance and practices. Eventually, we would bring these companies together in a series of workshops to confirm our findings.

On its own, however, this process was insufficient. We recognized that to be generic our study would need to extend beyond these five organizations. We therefore set about broadly testing our findings using two mechanisms, namely:

1. Organizing a further nine case studies. These were manufacturers that were also following a servitization strategy, but not as mature in their progress as our core collaborators. Identified through our initial survey work (section 4.1), we would use these companies to contrast and test (rather than generate) the findings arising from our core collaborators.

2. Engaging the broader research and practitioner community. Systematically we held hundreds of conversations and private briefings with managers and engineers, along with workshops, conferences and industry forums. We also contributed to academic

conferences and journals, and received feedback from the respective research communities on our contributions.

In all, this process extended over five years. In the following sections we present the culmination of this research, and pay particular attention to the practices and technologies applied by those manufacturers leading in the delivery of advanced services. First, however, we set these in perspective by summarizing the characteristics typical to conventional production operations.

5.2 A Perspective Against the World of Production

The world of production provides a reference point. In this section we set out some of the key features of this world to express the starting point for conventional manufacturers embarking on servitization.

Production operations are synonymous with factories: centralized facilities, created to exploit economies of scale and resource availability and so inexpensively deliver large numbers of high-quality products; and people and equipment co-located within large facilities, with production materials being brought to the location and finished products leaving.

The size and location of factories vary. Much depends on whether the manufacturer is producing low volumes of large and complex products, or high volumes of fast moving consumer goods. Factors such as demand, labour, materials, proximity of markets, market access and government incentives all have an impact. Within operations, needs for low product cost, high quality and short/reliable lead-times explain many of the practices and technologies that occur.

Driven by such factors, manufacturers flex their vertical integration. Modern production facilities are significantly less vertically integrated than their predecessors. For example, when Henry Ford commenced production of the Model T in the early twentieth century his factories contained many of the production processes necessary for the construction of his automobile. This was necessary in order to control quality conformance, which in turn helped to minimize the overall costs. Since then improvements in capabilities within the supply base have relaxed the need for such extensive vertical integration. Concepts such as core competences have motivated manufacturers to divest and relinquish such integration. Many have outsourced a portion of their operations, only keeping in-house those capabilities that are critical to their control over cost, quality and delivery.

The technologies within production facilities have similarly evolved. These are dependent on the products being produced. Automotive plants will house robotics, conveyors and automatic assembly lines, whereas producers of complex aerospace components might focus more on machining and fabrication technologies. Again, across these cases the key drivers underpinning the developments of technologies have been cost, quality and delivery.

Nowhere has this rationale been more obvious than in the planning and control of production. Sophisticated information and communication technologies (ICTs) have been developed to ensure customer demands are satisfied with the minimum level of stockholding. Popular systems are Manufacturing Resource Planning (MRP II) and Enterprise Resource Planning (ERP). Both are integrated hardware and software applications linked to a central database that stores and delivers business data and information, facilitates the flow of information between all business functions inside the boundaries of the organization and manages the connections to external stakeholders.

People remain key to many production operations. Yet the type of people favoured in production environments, and the way they are commonly directed, again reflect demands of cost, quality and delivery. For example, one of the principal innovations during the industrial revolution of the 1700s was the assembly line. Here, relatively unskilled men and women were trained to do a single task on a product, then, having done so, move it along to the next worker. In this way they significantly increased their output over artisans in the conventional craft-based systems. Henry Ford is well known for using such systems to revolutionize automotive manufacture.

Finally, the organizational processes within factories focus on efficiency and consistency. For instance, the quality standards of ISO 9000 and 9001 seek to ensure that all processes are in place to ensure production standards are maintained. Many such processes are initiated with customer orders and conclude at the products' 'point of sale'. Customers tend to be dealt with transaction by transaction. Such processes are less effective at dealing with, for instance, after-sales services. They tend to be reactive to such demands.

A picture of conventional production operations therefore emerges. When considering servitization, many manufacturers start from a position of: centralized production facilities; measures focused on cost, quality and delivery; systems focused on the planning and control of production; and people and processes that emphasize efficiency and consistency leading up to the 'point of sale'. These features are captured in Table 5.1, and set out a challenging starting position should a manufacturer seek to follow a servitization strategy.

5.3 Advanced Services and Product–Service Systems

Most people hold a fairly clear understanding of a factory – a building housing machines and people that come together to transform materials and produce a product. Although a rather simplistic view, it quite rightly distinguishes between the production system and the product. Unfortunately clarity is often absent in any equivalent discussions around services and their delivery.

Table 5.1 Features of conventional production operations

Aspect of production operations	Typical characteristics
Overall focus	Transactional sale; operations focus on minimizing production costs, ensuring quality conformance, and delivery
Performance measures	Focused on cost, quality and delivery of products
Facilities and their location	Centralized to exploit economies of scale, natural resources and proximity to markets
Vertical integration	Integrated where needed to control cost and quality
Information and communication technologies	Focused on the planning and control of material flow
People deployment and skills	Staff who are technically excellent, analytical and highly reliable
Business processes	Reactive to demands for after-sales support and tendency towards 'heroic recovery'

So far in this book, we have introduced and explained servitization and advanced services. We have emphasized that advanced services are distinctive because they focus on delivering a capability for the customer. The term 'product–service system' (PSS) is generally given to the broader mechanism or 'system' that delivers these advanced services. In this section we explore the generic structure of such a system.

The term product–service systems (PSS) largely originated from Scandinavia and northern Europe (section 2.5). Originally promoted from a sustainability perspective, it has gained traction in recent years as a term for describing the system that comes together to deliver advanced services. Also popular in this context is the term 'service delivery system'. A PSS can be thought of as comprising a 'service delivery system' (i.e. the operations of the manufacturer), plus any financial systems (i.e. financial leasing) and supplier systems (i.e. supply of consumables).

Product–service systems support a vast range of 'touch-points' that collectively define the 'customer experience'. In the world of production there are relatively few 'touch-points' as the emphasis is firmly on the product sale transaction. Longer-term relationships with customers are, of course fostered, but these simply result in sale transactions being repeated. Advanced services extend these touch-points beyond the point of sale and throughout the life-cycle of the contract. They begin with the interactions of sales personnel, technicians and project managers at the generation and deployment of a contract, and stay in place throughout the execution and delivery of this contract.

A typical PSS is illustrated in Figure 5.1. This shows how such a system may appear in a rail industry example. Here, the customer

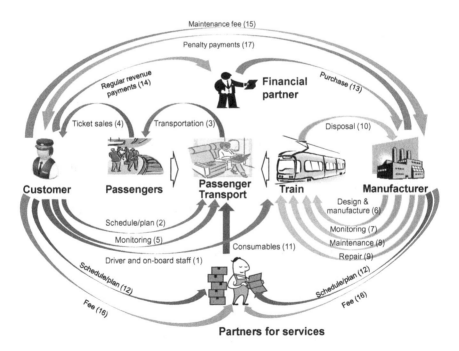

Figure 5.1: *Principal interactions in a PSS delivering an advanced Service*

would be a train operator such as FirstGroup or Tube Lines (operators of the London Underground Northern Line) who seek to contract for the availability and use of trains rather than their conventional purchase. Manufacturers such as Alstom would then contract to provide trains and rolling stock, along with all the maintenance and support activities necessary to ensure the availability and reliability contracted with the operator. The customer (or train operator), manufacturer and their partners all have through-life interactions with each other and the product (occasionally referred to as the asset). These interactions are illustrated by the line arrows in the diagram. Such a system operates in the following way.

The customer is focused on the use of the capability to transport passengers. They have to provide some resources (1) to use the capability, such as train drivers, managers, and on-board staff. They also place a demand signal on the train, in this instance, by providing a schedule/plan for the train journey (2). In return the customer receives the benefits that the capability provides. In this instance the transportation of rail passengers (3). They, themselves, translate this benefit into financial income through the sales of tickets, and on train services such as refreshments (4). Invariably the customer monitors how well the capability is being provided (5) using measures that directly relate to their own business model. These may be, for example, the extent of any train delays that their passengers experience on the rail network.

The manufacturer not only provides the design, manufacture and installation of the train itself (6) but also, frequently, takes responsibility for this being available for use (one of the key features we discussed in section 3.4). Consequently, they monitor the performance of the train (7), and carries out maintenance (8) and repair (9), to ensure this availability. The manufacturer may also be responsible for the disposal (10) of the equipment should this need to be replaced during the lifetime of the contract.

Both the customer and manufacturer may engage partners to provide support services. Typically, these may be consumables such as fuel or catering consumables (11). These are initiated either by schedules or plans (12) either from the customer or manufacturer, depending on the nature of their contractual agreements.

Financial processes are also included in this system. Table 3.4 in Chapter 3 illustrates how these may typically occur. The financial partner provides the funds that enable the product purchase (13), and in return receives regular revenue payments (14) that reflect the usage of the capability by the customer. The customer also pays a similar regular fee for train maintenance (15) to the manufacturer. Both the customer and manufacturer might also make payments to their partners for any additional services they have consumed. However, should the train fail to perform in anyway, such that the capability is not available to the customer, then the manufacturer may be liable for financial penalties (17).

5.4 Service Delivery System for Advanced Services

Throughout this study our underlying ambition has been to develop a thorough understanding of how to deliver advanced services successfully. For us a key question has been; *what are the practices and technologies within operations that enable a PSS to work well, and deliver advanced services successfully?* But as Figure 5.1 illustrates, a PSS contains a broad set of interactions. Some of these are beyond the scope of our study such as the processes associated with the financial partners.

Our specific interest is the mechanism for service delivery, in other words the 'service delivery system'. This is the interaction of practices and technologies, within the broader operations of the manufacturer, that come together to deliver the service offering. We are, however, sparing in our use of the term service delivery system. Practitioners within conventional manufacturers are more familiar with terms such as operations, and operations strategy, and so we favour this language.

The importance of a systems view is well understood in operations management. Authors such as Richard Schonberger performed a study similar to ours in the early 1980s, and looked closely at Just-in-Time within the Kawasaki motorcycle plant in Lincoln, Nebraska, USA. Similarly, Jim Womack, Dan Jones and Dan Roos carried out an equivalent study of Lean production at Toyota. In both cases they set out to rationalize and reduce the systems they studied into discrete components (e.g. Kanban, Kaizen), such that they could then describe and communicate their findings to the wider audience. Yet they always recognized that organizations such as Kawasaki and Toyota had created tightly coupled systems. All these elements needed to be implemented for the benefits to be realized.

Our approach is similar. We have rationalized and reduced our description of the system that manufacturers use to deliver advanced services successfully into six elements. As we examine shortly, these concern (1) facilities and their location, (2) micro-vertical integration and supplier relationships, (3) information and communication technologies, (4) performance measurement and the demonstration of value, (5) people deployment and their skills, and (6) business processes and relationships. To succeed, however, these practices and technologies need to be integrated as a tightly coupled system. We illustrate this interaction with Figure 5.2. Factors external to this system also impact on success, and these include:

- *Characteristics of the advanced service offering:* In much the same way that a product might be poorly suited to an application, an advanced service offering can be inappropriate for a customer's needs. No

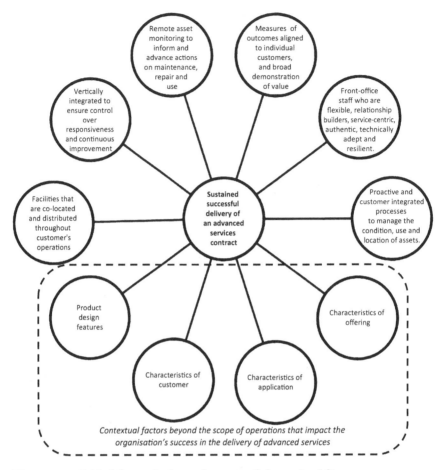

Figure 5.2: *Critical factors in the performance of the service delivery system*

matter how well the manufacturer fulfils the capabilities specified, these are simply insufficient or too extensive.

- *Characteristics of the customer and application:* Some customers may fail to use the product (or equipment) as specified in the contract. With power-by-the-hour, for instance, contracts are negotiated for aircraft according to the routes they use. Should a customer fail to adhere to these it may be penalized; if it persists then relationships begin to break down and eventually the contract can become unworkable.

- *Product design features:* Advanced services can only go some way to accommodating poor product designs. For instance, should a product continually fail in service because it is simply unsuited to an application, then the financial burden on the manufacturer can eventually mean that the contract is not viable.

We will return to discuss these factors further in the conclusion section. Our focus from now on will be on the service delivery system.

5.5 Key Capabilities of a Service Delivery System

Earlier we explained how production systems tended to focus on delivering a large number of high-quality products inexpensively. Another way of looking at this is that successful factories have 'capabilities' that underpin their performance against quality, cost and delivery. The practices and technologies that they use in production reflect these capabilities.

There are, therefore, capabilities that begin to explain the practices and technologies that successful manufacturers use to deliver advanced services. They form a common thread running through the service delivery system. Those organizations that exhibit these most strongly are likely to be the better performers.

Understanding the nature of such capabilities is challenging. This term 'capability' is itself used rather loosely among both researchers and practitioners, and it is easy to be drawn into describing a myriad of features of service delivery systems. This we sought to avoid in our study. Our goal was simply to understand the key practical abilities, within operations, that a company has to have in place if it is to succeed in delivering advanced services.

As our study progressed, time and time again we reflected on this challenge. Slowly two capabilities emerged from our investigation:

- An ability to respond cost effectively.

- An ability to improve cost effectiveness.

It's easy to appreciate why a manufacturer has to be able to respond. Contracts for advanced service are defined using measures that directly relate to the customer's business. If the manufacturer fails, the customer fails.

Alstom ilustrates this in practice. Contracts with Virgin, and subsequently FirstGroup, are such that Alstom is penalized if its trains fail to perform as expected. There are tight tolerances on the amount of delays these customers will accept. Should a failure unexpectedly occur, Alstom needs to have the people, systems and spare parts in place to get the machine back in operation as soon as possible. The same is true for Rolls-Royce holding a power-by-the-hour contract with Singapore Airlines, or Xerox providing printing capability for Fiat. Such response has to be delivered efficiently. In all these examples, Alstom, Rolls-Royce and Xerox have to provide their advanced services profitably. They have to fulfil their contractual commitments with the minimum of manpower, materials and facilities.

A capability to improve continuously is also necessary. Such improvements enable cost reductions throughout the lifetime of an advanced services contract, and so ongoing improvements in profitability. Improvements can be made to both products and processes. Products can be redesigned so that they are more reliable, easier to maintain and faster to repair should they fail. Similarly, processes can be redesigned to deal proactively with failures, ensure a rapid response and minimize the manpower and materials necessary should a failure occur.

Intriguingly, an ability to improve begins to explain why those organizations with design and production expertise are well suited to deliver advanced services. They can instigate both forms of improvements. This gives them an edge over more pure-service providers such as third party logistics (3PL) providers.

3PL providers can be efficient in the process of supply chain management. However, the manufacturer has the means and authority to remove the need to rely on the supply chain. If a component breaks unexpectedly or fails prematurely the manufacturer can alter the design to reduce the chances of this happening again. Alstom refers to this process as exploiting a 'return on experience'. An excellent example of this is the air-conditioning units on the UK's West Coast Mainline (see section 8.4).

Improvements in design can bring about drastic improvements. Some Alstom managers predict that they may be able to make as much as 70% of their costs savings through ongoing product design rather than process improvements alone. Neither is it simply a case of the 3PL provider engaging a partner to re-engineer and reproduce parts; it is unlikely to hold the expertise to observe a failure and translate this meaningfully.

This interplay between a 'capability to respond' and a 'capability to improve' is a common thread or pillar underpinning the practices and technologies we discuss shortly, and explains how the capabilities of the manufacturers differ to the other forms of organizations we've mentioned. The matrix in Figure 5.3 positions organizations using these. Organizations positioned in the top right-hand quarter have the capabilities necessary to deliver advanced services successfully; they have both the knowledge and capacity as an organization to be sufficiently responsive to customer needs, while also improving their efficiency in delivering their response.

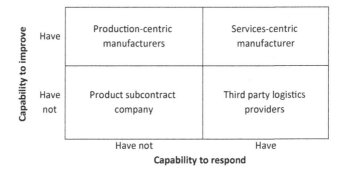

Figure 5.3: *Positioning organizations relative to capabilities needed to support advanced services*

5.6 Chapter Summary

To summarize, products are delivered by production systems; advanced services are delivered by product–service systems (PSS). In this chapter we have established the key terminology and described the typical structure of a PSS, and then focused on a subset of this system that is responsible for service delivery. This we refer to as the service delivery system. We have explained the scope of such a system, and the two critical capabilities that such a system should exhibit to be successful. From this platform we can examine the technologies and practices that are adopted by those manufacturers that are successfully delivering advanced services.

Chapter 6

PERFORMANCE MEASURES AND DEMONSTRATION OF VALUE

Production tends to focus on cost, quality and delivery. From one factory to the next these are prominent measures that feature strongly in conversations, performance charts and overall reporting procedures. Such measures begin to explain the practices and technologies apparent within many production operations. Consequently, in our study of servitized manufacturers we set out to find an equivalent system.

Initially we thought we had found such an equivalent in the measures of product (or asset) performance, availability and reliability. Once again, however, we were being influenced by our production heritage. We had naturally sought product-centric measures and expected them to be the same from one organization to the next. Eventually we appreciated that the world of the servitized manufacturer is very different. We have captured our principle finding as follows:

> **Principle 1**: Successful delivery of advanced services is enabled by measures focused on the outcomes aligned to individual customers, which are then cascaded in various forms throughout the service delivery system of the manufacturer, and complemented by indicators that broadly demonstrate value.

In this chapter we present what we now understand about the way in which leading adopters of advanced services measure their own performance. We begin by explaining how the business processes of the customer provide a principal set of measures which are then cascaded throughout operations in various forms. Each of these forms is then described more fully.

6.1 A Pyramid of Performance Measures

Our study revealed a pyramid of performance measures associated with an advanced services contract. All of the companies we studied held at the top layer of this pyramid a set of performance measures that were specific to the particular advanced services offering. From this layer measures were then cascaded into various forms to control the performance of operations and demonstrate value to the customer (Figure 6.1). In this section we describe the overall structure of this pyramid, and in the following sections examine each layer in detail.

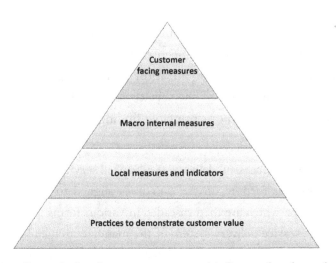

Figure 6.1: *Pyramid of performance measures and indicators for advanced services*

At the highest level of the pyramid the performance measures are 'those of the customer'. They reflect the business processes of the customer that are supported by the advanced services contract. We refer to these as the 'customer facing measures'.

Customer facing measures sit at the interface or boundary between the customer operations and the service operations of the manufacturer. On the customer's side of this boundary performance is assessed in terms of measures that relate directly to the customer's own business processes. On the other side is the service delivery system of the manufacturer. The positioning of this boundary in a typical product–service system (PSS) is illustrated in Figure 6.2.

Within the manufacturer's service delivery system the customer facing measures are then translated into a set of 'macro internal measures'. These are more meaningful for the manufacturer in the way

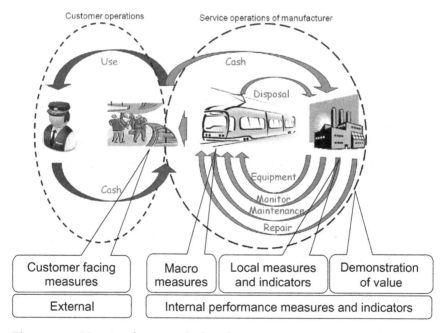

Figure 6.2: *Mapping the pyramid of performance measures onto a product–service system*

they relate to the product (asset) and process performance. For instance, if the customer facing measures relate to 'how long train passengers are waiting', then the macro internal measures might target 'train speed' (asset performance) and 'breakdowns' (asset availability and reliability).

These macro measures are then further deconstructed into local measures and indicators. These are used by the manufacturer to control all the subprocesses involved in the management of service delivery. For example, they may capture the number of faults recorded on a train or aircraft between scheduled maintenance activities. Alternatively, these might be standard times for carrying out maintenance activities, and indicators such as variance from these times.

Within these internal measures there is a second set of performance measures that reflects the expectations of the manufacturer's shareholders. Their demands for a return on investments translate into pressures to deliver services economically. Costs are measured in various ways, such as direct manpower and resources consumed, and indirectly as management ratios which indicate effectiveness and efficiencies in contract delivery.

At the base of the pyramid is a selection of measures that help to demonstrate value. These are somewhat softer and more emotional indicators that help to reassure customers about the capabilities and achievements of the manufacturer. These can occur in various forms across the service operations of the manufacturer.

6.2 Customer Facing Measures of Performance

Customer facing measures are distinct because they:

- Reflect the customer's own processes and how these are measured.

- Focus on the outcomes from a product's use rather than its delivery and sale.

- Tend to be specific to individual contracts and so difficult to generalize.

The emphasis on the customer's processes and measures is key. They focus on outcomes that are relevant to the customer's core business. For example, in the case of Alstom, the contract for London Underground Northern Line is managed on the basis of 'lost passenger hours'. These measures are those of their customer, and specifically meaningful to the operation of their business. For Caterpillar and their dealers, an equivalent contract would be with a customer engaged in quarrying and ore extraction, and so measures could be in terms of 'tonnes of material (ore and overburden) mined'. Other examples of customer facing measures are given in Table 6.1.

Table 6.1 Examples of customer facing measures

Advanced service example	Measure	Description
Alstom, London Underground Northern Line	Lost passenger hours	Extent of train delay (minutes), multiplied by number of passengers affected
Fleet management, MAN	Miles travelled	Total miles travelled by truck fleet
Document management, Xerox	Pay-per-copy	Price of individual paper copies
TotalCare, RR	Dollar per flying hour	Price per hour that engine is flown
MARC agreement, Caterpillar dealers	Dollar per tonne	Price per tonne of material mined

Such measures are set out at the formation of the contract and will last for its duration (i.e. five, ten and even 20 or more years). They are not normally renegotiated, unless serious problems occur with contract fulfilment, or some compensation is built into the contract to deal with components becoming obsolete and no longer maintainable (referred to as an obsolesences watch and occuring particularly with micro-process or hardware).

6.3 Macro Internal Measures of Performance

The manufacturer has the task of managing its operations to fulfil the customer facing measures. To achieve this they deconstruct these into a set of internal measures that are better suited to their products and processes.

Macro performance measures are, by comparison, more standardized across organizations. For instance, on advanced services contracts Caterpillar dealers, Alstom and MAN will all be concerned with the performance, availability and reliability of their vehicles. A typical interpretation of these measures is given in Figure 6.3.

The figure illustrates how these three measures may be interpreted for a single cycle of an asset's operation (in this case a 24-hour cycle). To explain, scheduled availability is concerned with the proportion of the time that an asset/product is intended to be accessible for use (in this case 20 hours). Here, there will be a corresponding period of scheduled downtime where planned maintenance occurs.

This may be factored to reflect the number of assets/products concerned. For example, on the West Coast Mainline the Alstom contract with Virgin is to have 47 Pendolino trains ready at the beginning of each day, and ensure that each of these trains will be available for 18 hours of that day. Availability can also be thought of as either scheduled or actual, to reflect the capacity intended against that realized in practice.

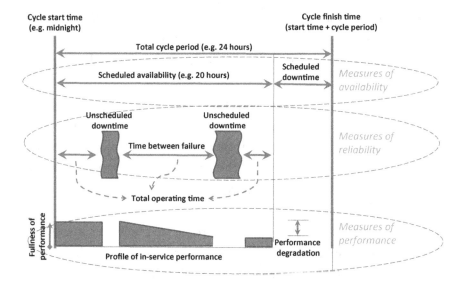

Figure 6.3: *Illustration of customer facing measures commonly used with advanced services*

If availability is concerned with the asset being ready for use, then reliability is an evaluation of in-service failures/unintended downtime. This is indicated by the frequency (time between failures) and duration of failures (unscheduled downtime) that occur during the time when an asset is scheduled to be available for use.

This downtime is the sum of the time that a manufacturer takes to respond to an in-service failure and the associated time to make good any necessary repairs. Spread over time, this can be measured in terms of the mean time between failure (MTBF) and the mean time to repair (MTTR).

Both the duration of a downtime and also when this occurs are important. With the London Underground Northern Line, for example, reliability is measured in terms of 'lost passenger hours'. These hours are calculated to reflect the overall impact on people if an underground train fails in service at differing times of the day and at a specific location on the network. Hence, a delay of five minutes at 8.30 am on a weekday at a key hub incurs a greater number of 'lost passenger hours' than a 30 minute delay at 9 pm on a Sunday evening at a network terminus.

Performance is concerned with the extent to which the specified capability of an asset is accessible during the scheduled availability. For example, this may be a measure of thrust available from a gas turbine (compared with that specified at the onset of the contract), or the speed at which a quarry truck can ascend a haul road when fully laden (again compared with that specified).

In Figure 6.3, this is illustrated as a profile that indicates the extent of asset performance, and how this may vary throughout the period of scheduled availability. Here, the asset will still be in use, but penalties are likely to be incurred by the manufacturers for the degradation of performance.

These three measures are clearly inter-related. A degradation of performance could be considered as an issue with both reliability and availability. For example, if a non-critical subsystem of an asset (e.g. an air-conditioning unit) has faults and does not work properly, then this could be interpreted as being both unreliable (if it failed in service) and unavailable (if it was not working at the beginning of the cycle). Similarly, if the asset fails completely in service (i.e. a reliability issue) then clearly it is unavailable for use.

These inter-relationships help to explain why advanced services are sometimes referred to simply as availability contracts. It appears helpful, however, to distinguish between the three failure modes explicitly and we summarize these definitions in Table 6.2.

Measures such as availability, reliability and performance directly relate to fulfilling customer commitments. The cost of contract fulfilment is also a key measure. This cost is the sum of the materials, manpower and resources that the manufacturer expends in delivering the advanced services contract.

Table 6.2 Failure modes associated with macro-internal performance measures

Failure mode	Termed as an issue with:	Excludes:
If asset is not ready for use	Availability	Fails in service and/or failure to fully perform as expected
If asset fails in service	Reliability	Asset not ready for use and/or failures to fully perform as expected
If an asset has faults and fails to fully perform as expected	Performance	Asset not ready for use and/or asset fails in service

6.4 Local Internal Measures and Indicators of Performance

The macro internal performance measures are then deconstructed into a set of internal measures to control the subprocesses within the service delivery system. These can be thought of as a dashboard for the assessment and management of advanced services contracts, and are expressed in terms of the time taken for contract fulfilment, costs incurred in achieving these and monitoring of any variances.

Standard times and variance from these is particularly important. Manufacturers will typically assess the time taken by subprocesses to deliver service offerings, for example the time taken to carry out a scheduled maintenance procedure. These then define the workload and time taken for subprocess. By combining the profiles for all the subprocesses, the overall effort and resources to deliver an advanced services contract can be determined.

Variance from these standard times is a critical measure. Not only might it mean that more resources, such as manpower and materials, are required to carry out a service activity, it may also mean that the manufacturer holds a greater risk of failing to fulfil availability metrics. These can themselves incur substantial penalties.

These measures may be further translated into indicators that relate to the overall efficiency and effectiveness of contract delivery. These more general ratios also allow contract-by-contract comparisons. Certain ratios that are particularly common among our case companies.

Overall asset effectiveness, for example, relates to the extent of downtime (both scheduled and unscheduled) that occurred over a period of asset operation. Typically this can be calculated as shown below, with a high efficiency being registered if the number of faults is low.

$$\text{Overall Asset Effectiveness} = (\text{Total Operating Time}/(\text{Total Operating time} + \text{Total Downtime})) \times 100\%$$

Overall asset utilization indicates the extent to which an asset has been used compared with that expected. The importance of this indicator will be affected by the form of an advanced service. In particular, high asset utilization may be especially desirable with a pay-for-use contract as a direct link can be made with revenue generation. This indicator is typically calculated as:

$$\text{Overall Asset Utilization} = (\text{Operating Time}/\text{Scheduled Availability}) \times 100\%$$

Overall asset availability is calculated in a similar way, and indicates the extent to which the asset was available for use. Again, a high value is taken as an indication of success.

$$\text{Overall Asset Availability} = (\text{Actual Availability}/\text{Scheduled Availability}) \times 100\%$$

The overall maintenance ratio is calculated in a similar way and indicates the amount of effort required to ensure the asset is both reliable and available. This therefore takes into account both the actual time for asset maintenance (which will occur during the period of scheduled downtime) and the total downtime brought about by in-service failures. This total is itself a function of the time to respond and repair a failure, and the frequency with which such repairs are needed. This can be calculated as follows, and in this instance a low value is desirable.

Overall Maintenance and Repair Ratio

$= f$(Actual Time for Scheduled Asset Maintenance

$+$ Unscheduled Downtime)/ Operating Time) $\times 100\%$

These four indicators focus on how well an advanced services contract is being fulfilled. The time and money consumed in achieving this (and therefore the internal efficiency) can be assessed by a number of other measures, and ultimately these can be captured by one cost indicator.

These principal measures include maintenance and repair costs (concerned with the labour and materials consumed in making repairs), stockholding costs (concerned with the cost of holding spare parts and consumables) and infrastructure/overhead costs (such as rent and leases on facilities, management costs).

In addition, costs occur in the form of penalties if there are failures to fulfil the contracted performance, availability and reliability. These four costs combine to give the overall cost of contract delivery. It is then possible to consider these against the revenue received, and in this way generate the gross margin for the contract or in other words the overall contract contribution. This structure can be illustrated as:

Overall Cost of Contract Delivery

$= f$(Maintenance and Repair Costs $+$ Stockholding Costs

$+$ Infrastructure and Overhead Costs $+$ Penalties)

Overall Contract Contribution

$$= f(\text{Revenue Earned} - \text{Overall Cost of Contract Delivery})$$

Collectively the measures and indicators provide a means for the manufacturer to assess how well a contract is being fulfilled and the costs of achieving this. In addition to these tangible measures of performance, there are a number of informal indicators that are employed to demonstrate to the customer the value being delivered by an advanced services contract. These are explored in the following section.

6.5 Demonstration of Value

Demonstration of value is critically important. In many respects advanced services are similar to insurance policies. If the customer sees that the manufacturer's product is working well, all of its performance measures are being fulfilled, and little indication that the manufacturer is having to work hard to fulfil these, then, over time, may question the benefits of an advanced service contract.

Unfortunately, the very nature of these contracts means that the activities of the manufacturer are largely unseen. This situation was succinctly captured by a senior manager at Rolls-Royce who said, *'If the customer doesn't see what they are getting, they think they are getting nothing.'* Those manufacturers that are successful in their delivery of advanced services have also developed a selection of practices that focuses on demonstrating value to customers.

Many of these practices are quite subtle. These manufacturers are not creating new activities, but rather carefully presenting those activities that are already being performed. The activities are themselves critical to the delivery of the advanced services offering. It is simply a case of ensuring that the customer appreciates how hard the manufacturer is working.

Control rooms provide an excellent example. Early in the programme we were invited to observe a control room that was being used to manage a variety of advanced services contracts (we will examine these facilities in more detail shortly). Not having seen such facilities within production environments, we initially stood a little awestruck as we observed banks of computers, engineers and central display screens. Intrigued, we paid close attention to what we saw and asked many questions of our guide, and so came to observe the control room for perhaps a little longer than other visitors may do.

We began to realize that the control room was a little less dynamic than we had initially supposed. We became aware that the only consciously updated display screen seemed to be the one showing the BBC newsfeeds. This is not to suggest that the control room was not fulfilling its purpose, but rather that there was an element of 'showing off'. The glass partitions, location of the facility, and number of display screens, all added to the impact of the facility.

This experience heightened our awareness of practices that help to demonstrate value to the customer. We now examine these more closely.

Demonstrate value by presenting operations, war and training rooms that illustrate investment and complexity

Delivery of advanced services benefits from well-designed control rooms or war rooms, along with well-trained maintenance staff. In operations rooms, frontline staff are co-located with the various information technologies that help them deliver advanced services contracts. These can include technologies that feed back the locations and condition of an asset, performance metrics and schedules, and

Enterprise Resource Planning systems that present resource and stock-holding availability.

Located in such facilities are project managers, condition monitoring technicians, maintenance planning personnel and staff responsible for communications with customers and partners. A good example of such a facility is at Rolls-Royce Aerospace in Derby where typically 3000 gas turbines are monitored continuously and their maintenance strategies are organized.

Control rooms tend to be staffed constantly to deal with operational issues. War rooms are used on a more occasional basis for tactical and strategic monitoring and decision making. The latter will have a bias towards presentation of metrics rather than being equipped for the day-to-day management of contracts. Both facilities tend to be open plan, incorporating large display screens which are continuously updated by streamed data, enclosed by a glass surround, and favourably located for optimum visibility to visitors to the facility.

Staff training facilities can have a similar role. One of our cases had a particularly well-equipped training room, with many examples of potential equipment faults and failures that can be caused by poor maintenance. This training room was again located close to the visitors' entrance. When questioned as to whether this facility was to train customer technicians as well as their own, the response from the manufacturer was quite clear '*no, it's to scare them!*' In other words, educating the customer continually about the effort required to fulfil an advanced services contract provides a useful tactical device.

Demonstrate value by presenting well-organized maintenance facilities to show capability

A challenge that many manufacturers face is to demonstrate to the customer that they are better positioned to deliver services than either the customer themselves or their current suppliers. This is especially important with more traditional customers who are themselves experienced in the delivery of services.

The judgement of such customers will be informed by their observations at maintenance facilities. Customers will be reassured when they see that facilities are suitably laid out, repair areas are clearly defined, regulation awareness and conformance are clearly apparent, staff planning is in place and there is an ample stockholding.

Ironically, a competitive advantage that manufacturers have when they move to advanced services is that they can reduce stockholding by utilizing their production capabilities. Nevertheless, experienced customers may be reassured when they observe that adequate stock is available and suitably located, and the manufacturer can therefore demonstrate value in this way.

Further value is demonstrated when the brand and origin of such spare parts and consumables are clearly apparent. In one of our cases, the spare parts warehouse was laid out such that those components where the manufacturer's own brand was most clearly visible on packaging (e.g. lubrications filters, hydraulic oil drums) were most easily seen by visitors to the facility.

Demonstrate value by communicating regularly the activities being carried out

Many of our cases communicated regularly with their customers, and in part this was to remind them of the activities the manufacturers were carrying out. A number of subtle tactics were employed, and efforts were made to engage personnel across the customer's organization. Rockwell, for example, will send out regular maintenance reports to customers which are then followed up by a courtesy call.

A Caterpillar dealership demonstrated this tactic very well. When performing scheduled maintenance activities on quarry trucks, field maintenance technicians would always arrive early and meet with the equipment operators. They would discuss the equipment performance and any faults emerging. In doing so, they would not only gain early warning of any issues with the equipment, but they would also demonstrate the resources that were being invested to support the services contract. Without this practice the actions of the field technician could have been invisible to the operator.

Demonstrate value by carefully orchestrating tours through facilities

During our study we visited very many facilities delivering advanced services. On occasions we became aware that the way the tours were being given followed similar programmes. Not to suggest that we were being manipulated, but rather that manufacturers had learnt that visitors were most impressed if tours followed certain routines. As our programme was executed we recorded the practices that manufacturers followed. These are summarized in Table 6.3.

6.6 Chapter Summary

Performance measures begin to explain the practices and technologies apparent within many manufacturers delivering advanced services. In this chapter we have described how advanced services lead to a performance measurement pyramid.

At the apex are measures that relate directly to the customer's processes within which the advanced service integrates. These are then cascaded through the manufacturer's service delivery system into various metrics that help to control and assess the efficiency and effectiveness of the manufacturer. At the base of this pyramid are a broad selection of more emotional measures that help to demonstrate to the

Table 6.3 Common practices for demonstrating value within operations

Topic	Policy	Typical practices
Arrival and reception	Promote positive first impression of facility and brand by guiding the visitor smoothly to the site and reception	1. Provide clear directions to the facility and reception area 2. Develop surrounding landscape and site/facility entrance to portray the brand image 3. Provide adequate parking 4. Consider that visitors may arrive by coach and if so provide adequate access 5. Display products and company's heritage in the reception area
Health and safety briefing	Treat health and safety briefings as an opportunity to demonstrate a positive image of the manufacturing facility	1. Promote both safety and business values at the health and safety briefing 2. Provide high visibility vests and safety glasses with company logo 3. Ensure that safety signage also carries company brand

(Continued)

Table 6.3 (*Continued*)

Topic	Policy	Typical practices
Introduce the role of the manufacturer	Introduce the role of manufacturer within the customer's business	1. Use video, interactive exhibits and displays to promote business successes 2. Present company history, splitting the story into eras for ease of understanding 3. Convey messages consistent with both present and future product and service strategies
Guiding visitors	Develop a pre-planned, well-guided and carefully managed route through the facility	1. Identify a preferred tour route 2. Assign experienced and enthusiastic tour guides 3. Support tour guides with communication aids 4. Avoid dirty or potentially hazardous areas 5. Control times when facility can be visited 6. Ensure high standards of housekeeping on route 7. Ensure visual aids and performance measurement boards are up to date
Presenting technologies and practices	Carefully exhibit exciting and engaging production processes that are consistent with brand values	1. Emphasize processes that support brand identity 2. Highlight technologies and practices that are memorable 3. Show only those activities that are consistent with brand values

Appearance of the workforce	1. Provide company apparel/uniforms in keeping with the brand
Portray a workforce appearance that is consistent with the brand values	2. Ensure workforce is courteous in the way it interacts with the visitors
	3. Raise workforce awareness of visitors through clothing (high visibility vests, etc.)
Appearance of the working environment	1. Adopt company colour schemes and logos throughout the production environment
Demonstrate a clean and orderly environment with subtle reminders of the brand identity	2. Ensure the working environment is clean and well organized
	3. Emphasize commitment to the environment?
Product and component placement	1. Exhibit completed products or parts at both the beginning and end of the tour
Make good use of product placement to provide link with brand	2. Incorporate semi-finished parts on storyboards
	3. Provide product samples
Departure from the facility	1. Offer a memento to remind visitors of the visit
Ensure that visitors 'take the brand home' when they leave	2. Provide a shop to allow visitors to purchase gifts

customer the complexity and resources that are associated with the delivery of advanced services contracts.

With this platform in place, we will now examine more closely the practices and technologies that are common to manufacturers that are succeeding in the delivery of advanced services contracts.

Chapter 7

Factory buildings are often taken for granted. When walking around an established production facility we rarely stop to ask *'why is it located here?'* Only when discussions arise about off-shoring production to lower labour cost economies do managers start to reflect on the rationale underpinning a factory's size and location.

Where facilities have existed in the same place for some time, or where ownership has been taken over by another company, this underlying rationale may seem lost. In every case, however, at some point in time, a good reason has existed for facilities being geographically located where they are today.

Occasionally these reasons are not what might be expected. For example, BMW build their Mini cars in the Cowley plant at Oxford, UK. *Why is the factory in this location?* They took over this facility from Rover, previously British Leyland, and previous to that Morris. Oxford was the home town of William Morris, the company founder.

There are, however, more clinical rationales underpinning the location of many production facilities. As we established earlier, the common practice is for factories to bring together people, equipment and materials in a centralized location that exploits economies of scale and resources. Simply put, the world of production is epitomized by large centralized facilities that set out to deliver large numbers of high-quality products inexpensively.

Does servitization impact the facilities of manufacturers? This question was at the forefront during our studies with Rolls-Royce, Alstom, MAN, Caterpillar (and dealers) and Xerox. We were particularly interested in how these changed, if at all, at a macro-level (we would examine new resources such as control centres later). We sought to understand whether location, size and number of facilities altered when the organization focused on delivering advanced services.

We recognized from the outset that answering these questions could be complex. We were mindful that historical factors (as with BMW) could explain the practices of some companies. Likewise, manufacturers (such as Rolls-Royce) would compete both through services and the conventional sale of products. The extent of such original equipment manufacture might again affect the practices we observed.

As our programme drew to a conclusion a clear picture did emerge. Gone was the emphasis on large and centralized facilities, instead the following principle explained what we saw:

> **Principle 2**: Successful delivery of advanced services is enabled by facilities that are co-located and distributed throughout customers' operations.

In this chapter we will explain this practice and why it is favoured, and summarize the factors that mitigate the impact.

7.1 Facilities in the Delivery of Advanced Services

When a manufacturer sets out to deliver advanced services their facilities are invariably impacted. The picture that emerges is of develop-

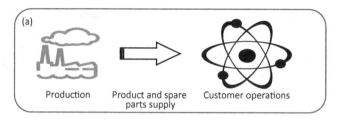

Figure 7.1a: *Production operations favour centralized production facility*

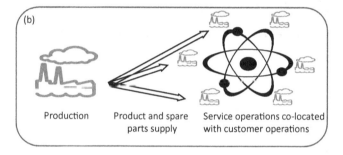

Figure 7.1b: *With advanced services the manufacturer develops (or adopts) operations co-located with those of the customer*

ment or adoption of smaller distributed facilities co-located with the operations of the customer. This difference is illustrated simplistically in Figures 7.1a and b.

The production worldview is shown in Figure 7.1a – a centralized production facility delivering products into the customer's operations. To deliver advanced services, Figure 7.1b, the manufacturer sets up or adopts service operations that are situated close to the operations of the customer.

Rolls-Royce Aerospace illustrates this practice in action. Their move to deliver power-by-the-hour contracts in civil aerospace has required them to extend their operations to engage in joint ventures in maintenance and repair facilities in Texas, Hong Kong and Singapore

Rolls-Royce pre-TotalCare
(operations located principally in the UK)

Rolls-Royce post-TotalCare
(operations located in the UK, USA,
Singapore and Hong Kong)

 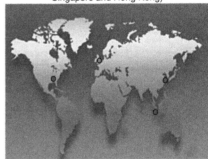

Figure 7.2: *Facilities of Rolls-Royce Aerospace before and after their move into advanced services*

(see Figure 7.2). Each location is strategically important to a key customer. Similarly, Caterpillar has an extensive geographic network of closely coupled dealers, and these dealers themselves may have strategically placed depots close to the customer base. MAN is somewhat similar, again facilities are carefully located geographically such that they are physically close to their principal customer base. In the London region, for example, facilities are typically within a ten mile radius of the customer (the vehicle operator).

The distributed facilities supporting advanced services are maintained in addition to centralized production facilities carrying out the design and manufacture of products. The picture that emerges is somewhat complex and has the following features:

1. Products that are sold conventionally are produced in centralized production facilities.
2. Products that form the basis of advanced services offerings are also produced in a centralized facility.
3. Advanced services which subsume products are delivered through facilities that are co-located with customers' operations.

Advanced services, therefore, don't mean that centralized production facilities are no longer necessary but that they are insufficient in themselves to deliver such services. Additional facilities that are located close to the customers' operations are also needed.

Distributed and co-located facilities are not unusual in service operations. Most manufacturers will have a network of distributors, dealers or partners for getting their products out to customers. Such distributors will have sales depots and repair shops carefully positioned so that they are easily accessible to customers.

The significance with advanced services is that the manufacturer has to have a bigger presence in these facilities. To put it quite bluntly, for a manufacturer to deliver and reap the rewards of an advanced services contract it has to be there! As we explore in the following section on vertical integration, manufacturers do much more in these facilities than simply distribute products.

This is exactly what has happened between Alstom and Virgin. Alstom designed and manufactured the Pendolino trains operated by Virgin Trains on the West Coast Mainline routes in the UK. As part of supporting this advanced service, they subsequently took over the existing track-side maintenance and repair facilities which are distributed regionally across the rail network.

Finally, it is difficult to decouple a discussion about facilities from the topics of vertical integration. Through servitization the manufacturer moves forwards in the supply chain to take over activities previously carried out by customers, and in doing so often adopts facilities within the customers' operations. We, however, treat facilities and vertical integration separately, mainly to ease our task of describing these practices, but also because these are separate decisions. A manufacturer could, for instance, attempt to provide advanced services from a single location. Conversely, they could adopt distributed facilities without moving into servitization. We will return to describe vertical integration practices in Chapter 8.

7.2 Impact of Facilities and Their Location

Smaller, distributed and co-located facilities forfeit the economies of a centralized plant, *so why are they necessary?* Quite simply, proximity aids responsiveness. Figure 7.3 illustrates how this occurs by showing how this practice relates to the internal performance measures that are typical of advanced services offerings (section 6.1). This relationship is explained as follows.

Localized facilities aid fault diagnosis and speed of repair (links 1 and 2 in Figure 7.3). This directly impacts product availability and may occur as a result of both faster fault diagnostics and response to a problem. This is achieved because staff are more likely to be on-hand when a failure occurs, possibly witnessing it themselves, and so can take corrective actions more quickly and precisely.

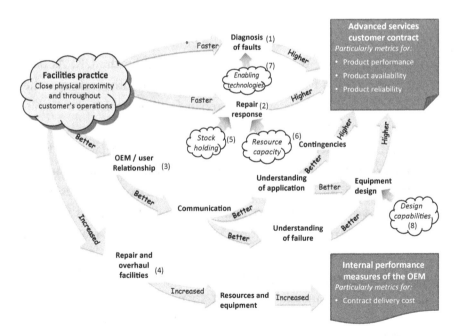

Figure 7.3: *Relationship between facilities practice and macro internal performance measures*

Examples of this in practice include Caterpillar dealers, who are likely to hold maintenance personnel and critical spare parts for quarry trucks on-site, in reserve and at large customer mines. Likewise, Alstom supports its activities on the London Underground Northern Line through safety stock, at line-side maintenance and repair facilities located at end-of-line stations.

The proximity of facilities also impacts positively upon reliability. Principally this is through a process that centres on building strong relationships between the manufacturer and customer at the level of day-to-day operations (3). This is critical to a healthy communication process, which itself enables the manufacturer to witness and directly improve their understanding of the application and the way in which the user operates their product.

This knowledge can be used to either arrange appropriate contingencies should failure occur (for example, knowing precisely where to locate stock reserves and so improving availability), or subsequently modify the design of products so that they become more reliable. Indeed, it is this capability to improve product designs that provides manufacturers with a significant advantage over competitors who are more conventional service providers.

Although positioning facilities throughout the customer's operations impacts positively upon performance, availability and reliability, the downside is that contract delivery costs also increase (4). Replicating facilities throughout a customer's network of operations is expensive and invariably means that manpower and equipment are duplicated and cannot be utilized to their fullest extent.

7.3 Mitigating the Need for Co-Location

As we examined the facilities of companies that lead in their delivery of advanced services, two questions continued to recur to us: *Does a manufacturer really need to be there? Can't the manufacturer deliver services more remotely and so regain some of the economies of scale we associate with production?* On completing this programme we concluded that, yes, this is possible – but only partially.

The need for co-located facilities is relaxed by other practices and technologies in the service delivery system. As illustrated in Figure 7.3, most significant are stockholding policies (5), available resource capacity (6), capabilities in remote product sensing technologies (7), and design capabilities (8). These factors impact the facilities practices in a number of ways.

Large amounts of capacity and stock can help to compensate, in part, for more remotely located facilities. If held centrally, with good distribution channels, replacement parts and consumables can be transported to locations where they are needed.

Information and communication technologies (Chapter 9) relax the need for co-location because they provide the manufacturer with advanced warning of an impending issue with an asset's performance. This can give time for people and equipment to travel to where the asset is located. Similarly, they can facilitate the remote repair of the asset by helping to diagnose the cause of any faults, and then remotely switching subsystems or advising the operator on compensating for problems.

Equipment design is also a critical factor. Modular designs, with relatively small size and cost, mean that it is feasible for maintenance technicians to replace faulty modules without attempting to repair them on-site. These can then be returned to central locations where they can then be overhauled. Similarly, self-heal technologies and reserve subsystems can all help to ensure that products are kept operational until they reach a centralized repair facility.

These practices and technologies can, however, only go partway to relaxing the need for co-located facilities. This is due in part to the limitations of information and communication technologies (we examine these in Chapter 9) and also to the customer's expectations of a 'demonstration of value'.

As we showed earlier, the demonstration of value is a somewhat emotional issue. In the case of facilities, there are expectations that the manufacturer will have presence. Facilities that are closely located give confidence in a capability to respond, especially if they are stocked with critical spare parts. Similarly, personal relationships are vitally important; indeed some see 'the field technician as the company's best sales person'. They can deal with issues locally, helping to prevent issues escalating.

A physical presence also has the advantage of increasing the customer's switching costs. Manufacturers can leverage additional business 'because they are there'. This is illustrated by companies such as Rolls-Royce, which has established joint ventures with key customers around the world. Setting up such facilities has been extremely expensive, but can provide an excellent platform to win business from new and existing customers in these locations.

7.4 Chapter Summary

In this chapter we have explored how the delivery of advanced services impacts the location, size and number of facilities needed by the manufacturer. There is pressure for facilities that are co-located and distributed throughout customers operations. In part this need is offset by stockholding policies, resource capacity, information and communication technologies, and design. Yet, no matter how advanced a manufacturer may be in each of these, pressures to demonstrate value mean that some physical presence in the customer's operations is almost always necessary.

Facility and vertical integration practices are closely coupled and so in the following chapter we will move on to the topic of vertical integration.

Chapter 8

VERTICAL INTEGRATION AND ORGANIZATIONAL STRUCTURE

Advanced services implicitly mean that the manufacturer moves forwards in their supply chain to carry out activities that were otherwise performed by the customer or their partners. In this sense, servitization and vertical integration are closely coupled topics. Yet changes to the boundary between the operations of the customer and manufacturer only go partway to explaining the impact of servitization on the vertical integration of the manufacturer.

Here, we use the term vertical integration for simplicity to capture the footprint of activities carried out by the manufacturer. Strictly speaking, this term is more usually associated with the ownership of businesses within supply chains rather than the activities of individual organizations. Terms such as span of process, strategic position, competitive space and micro-vertical integration are all similarly associated with this footprint of activities and can be substituted for the vertical integration terminology we use.

As we progressed with our research programme we could see how the physical facilities of manufacturers changed with their adoption of advanced services, and how the activities within these have previously been those of the customer. Yet the picture was not entirely clear. We sought to understand the range or span of activities in these facilities, and the competences being held in them by the servitized manufacturer. But we also sought to understand how the organizational structure of these manufacturers was changing and how these activities were impacted if the manufacturer was also engaged in conventional product sale and production.

Again, as our study unfolded we developed an understanding that we have captured in the principle below:

> **Principle 3**: Successful delivery of advanced services is enabled by integrating into a wide range of customer activities, through extensive front-office activities aligned around services offered, with design and production capabilities in place to support through life deployment.

In this chapter we will explain this practice and why it is favoured and summarize the factors that mitigate the impact.

8.1 Organizational Structure in the Delivery of Advanced Services

Taking the world of production as a starting point again, the organizational structure of centralized production facilities is influenced by whether the manufacturer is dealing with other businesses or directly with end consumers (B2B – business to business – or B2C – business to consumer). Those in the B2C world will probably use distributors to interface with customers, while in B2B this interaction is likely to be more direct.

In both instances, however, some form of sales office will exist to take care of those day-to-day customer interactions. Often this is referred to as the front office. The back office is the part of the business dedicated to running the company itself and typically includes people who deal with design, development, production and other activities that are rarely visible to customers.

In conventional manufacturing the front-office activities are relatively modest. They typically include marketing and promotion, sales order processing and dealing with enquires. They deal mainly with sales of new equipment and also spare or replacement parts. Orders for these parts are fulfilled by production and the customer then takes responsibility for using the equipment and, quite often, repairing it should it fail in service.

Figure 8.1 summarizes this organizational structure. The picture is of course more complex in many organizations, but this simple illustration helps to show the position taken by a typical production-centric manufacturer.

Advanced services move the manufacturer to take over customer operations as illustrated Figure 8.2. Front-office activities extend to include repair, maintenance, management and maybe even operation of the manufacturer's product. This is often coupled with the manufacturer developing the co-located facilities outlined in the previous section.

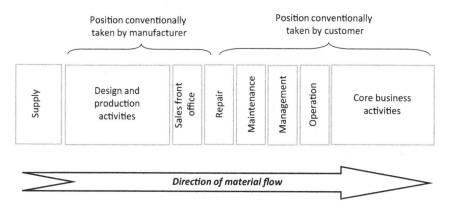

Figure 8.1: *Positioning of functions within a production-centric manufacturer and their customers*

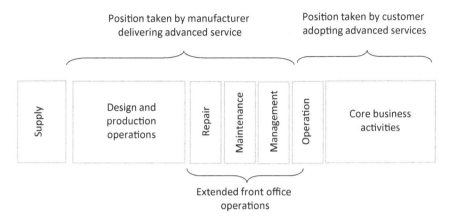

Figure 8.2: *Positioning of a servitized manufacturer and their customers for advanced services*

Alstom illustrates how this organizational restructuring can look in practice. British Rail was the train operator on the West Coast Mainline prior to Virgin. British Rail carried out the extended front-office operations (Figure 8.2) itself. With the transfer of this business to Virgin, these operations were taken over by Alstom, and they simultaneously took over track-side operations at five locations across this rail network including Wolverhampton, Glasgow, Manchester, Liverpool and Wembley. This left Virgin to focus on their core business activities such as marketing, ticket sales and train operation.

This restructuring brings about the 'organizational stretch' referred to in section 3.3. The manufacturer has to extend its responsibilities to manage the outcomes from the product's performance. Unfortunately this brings about internal complexities. For many manufactures, advanced services are delivered alongside other offerings, and tensions arise as the organization attempts to satisfy differing priorities.

Significant complications arise if the manufacturer remains engaged in conventional production and sale of products (base services). Customers of products hold differing expectations to those of advanced services, and so tensions arise between the responsibilities for production and service delivery systems. These are such that the organization splits and two somewhat independent business units are formed.

In this structure one part of the organization is production centric while the other is service centric. Externally this division of responsibilities can be difficult to see. Rolls-Royce, for example, initially appears as a single organization, but internal sub-businesses exist to support different markets and offerings. Unfortunately, simply splitting the organization into two parts rarely addresses all the tensions.

Further complications arise when the service-centric organization is also tasked with delivering a portfolio of services. In addition to advanced services, it focuses on intermediate services such as repair and overhaul, and base services such as product sale and distribution. Although the activities underpinning all offerings may be similar, their contractual priorities differ, which again bring about internal tensions within the organization. Service organizations respond to this by creating teams around each type of service offering, which are coordinated within a matrix-style management structure.

Figure 8.3 illustrates how this might appear for a typical organization delivering a portfolio of services. The width of the arrows signifies the relative priorities of base, intermediate and advanced services.

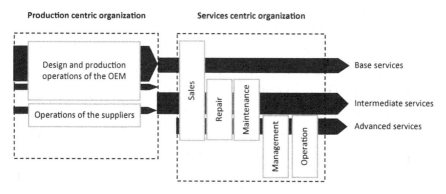

Figure 8.3: *Organizational structure and services (the differing line widths represent the typical importance of services within the two organizations)*

For production, the bulk of activities are focused on design and production of the base product, and to a much lesser extent spare and replacement parts. For the services organization, sales of such equipment might represent a much smaller portion of their focus. Spare parts are more significant, whether these are sold separately as base services, or consumed by maintenance and repair activities. Advanced services may only be a small portion of activities.

Complications can still arise if the service-centric organization restructures clinically around revenue flows. Revenue from base services, for example, might be relatively small, especially when a product has been sold at a discounted rate to gain services revenue. Such situations can lead to the service organization appearing highly profitable compared to production operations. This can be exaggerated if such revenues then influence investment priorities. Indeed, this can lead to product design and manufacture no longer being seen as important and the organization moving away from activities in this area.

Tensions are heightened when the production organization and the services organization are autonomous businesses. This is the situation faced by Caterpillar and its dealerships. Much of Caterpillar's revenue comes from the sale of products, parts and consumables through its dealers. When their dealers offer advanced services, Caterpillar can be reliant on the revenue from the base services that are consumed by the advanced services. However, because advanced services can push the costs for these base services back onto the dealership, the incentive is to reduce this consumption to a minimum, thus potentially reducing the revenue flow back to Caterpillar.

To succeed, the solution is a partnership in the delivery of advanced services. This includes restructuring the role of the production company and the revenue models within the service organization. Production can add value by exploiting competences in design and making sure that the products (and processes) are well suited to advanced services. For instance, improving the reliability and maintainability of products. Revenue is then apportioned back to production by following the same type of payment structure that the service organization sets up with the final customer (section 3.4).

A picture emerges, therefore, that to deliver advanced services successfully requires the manufacturer to develop an extended front-office function. Within this are teams that are aligned around differing types of services offerings but coordinated within a matrix-style management structure. As discussed in an earlier chapter, it's easy to envisage how these activities will take place in the facilities that are co-located with the customer's operations.

8.2 Vertical Integration in the Delivery of Advanced Services

When we examined the service operations of our case companies we didn't expect to see design and manufacture capabilities. Perhaps influenced by our background in production, we thought these would look like the garage facilities seen in automotive dealerships with sales personnel, maintenance technicians and repair capabilities. In every case, however, we observed mini-factories supporting the *deployment* of advanced services.

Alstom Train Life Services and Caterpillar dealerships illustrate this well. Alstom facilities on the West Coast Mainline had the capability to remanufacture and re-engineer the air-conditioning units for Pendolino trains. Similarly, Caterpillar dealerships could design and make subsystems for equipment, to help ensure suitability for particular applications. We, therefore, set out to question precisely the footprint of activities in the service operations.

At the outset we had chosen our case companies because they were manufacturers. These we defined by their authority for design and production. Our surprise, therefore, was not that the organization

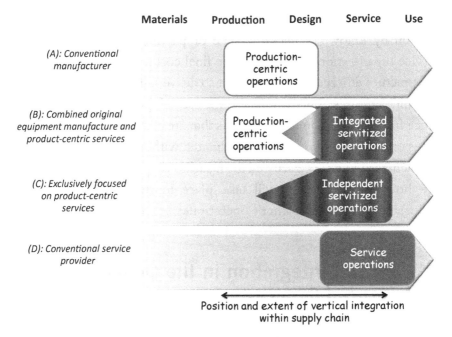

Figure 8.4: *Vertical integration practices in the delivery of advanced services*

held these capabilities, but that they extended into the services operations. Figure 8.4 sets out the footprint that operations take in these situations.

As illustrated in Figure 8.4 (A), the vertical integration of a conventional manufacturer tends to be arranged around design and production capabilities. Often basic services are offered, such as spare parts, but typically these are produced alongside normal production and delivered to the customer through a relatively independent network of dealers and distributors.

Such a model is often found in the automotive industry where manufacturers such as Toyota and Audi will have a franchised distributor network. Such distributors are themselves conventional service providers and offer a channel to the market for the manufacturer (see

(D) on Figure 8.4). Typically they will be entirely focused on services such as showrooms, demonstrations and sales.

The extent of vertical integration for servitization is somewhat blurred by the structure of the host organization. Manufacturers such as Rolls-Royce Aerospace, for example, initially appear to have extensive vertical integration. In practice, much of this is because the company is active in both original equipment manufacturer and product-centric services such as maintenance repair and overhaul (see (B) on Figure 8.4).

This tail of backward integration is illustrated in Figure 8.4 by a triangle penetrating design and production (see particularly (B) and (C)). Such integration exists even when conventional manufacture and product-centric servitization occur in one company (as per the case with Rolls-Royce). Here, there is both close integration and some duplication in activities. For example, both functions of such an organization may have assembly and test facilities. The extent of this penetration is, however, reduced, partly because some activities may be shared, and partly because of stronger supply chain leverage held by such a larger organization.

A more clinical picture of vertical integration supporting product-centric servitization is apparent in those companies that have focused entirely on servicing their existing installed asset base. These retain a tail of design and production capabilities (see (C) in Figure 8.4). Overall, this results in their operations being considerably extended.

This tail has been purposely retained rather than simply being a legacy of a move from production-centric operations. Alstom Train Life Services, for example, have intentionally reintegrated. Historically subsystems such as door actuators and coffee machines were sourced from external suppliers; more recently the overhaul and remanufacture of such equipment has been reintegrated into the Alstom organization. Though such facilities are not of the scale associated with conventional manufacture, both design authority and production capabilities have been established for these subsystems. Some of this reintegration is explained by the nature of the contractual relations that exist with suppliers, and deserves to be explored further.

In the production environment relationships with suppliers are frequently established in the early stages of product design. Suppliers are identified on the basis of their production capabilities and associated costs. Procurement processes are then executed that establish 'transactional'-style contracts. Here, support for through-life services tends to be limited to the longer-term provision of spare parts and consumables. Indeed, this is an important revenue stream for suppliers. Once again, however, transactional-style contracts are put in place.

Advanced services feature extensive contract life-cycles. The style of contract moves from transactional to a 'relationship' basis with the customer, and who then seek similar contracts with their own suppliers. Problems arise, however, when the contractual relationship with the supplier is 'transactional'.

The experiences of Alstom show how this can occur in practice. When the Pendolino trains were first designed and built the air-conditioning units were provided by an Austrian supplier. Transactional-style contracts were established. However, when these trains entered into use, as part of an advanced service between Alstom and Virgin, issues arose around the support that the supplier gave.

If units failed or needed overhaul they were sent back to the Austrian supplier. They performed the necessary activities competently, but were not able (or had little incentive) to respond quickly – unlike Alstom, of course, who were being measured on the performance of their trains; the functionality of air conditioning being an associated metric.

The consequence was that it was necessary to keep very significant amounts of stock were in the system. Costs increased, response suffered and the situation was not improving. Finally, Alstom reintegrated the manufacture (and subsequently re-engineering) of these air-conditioning units. Similar situations arose with a variety of subsystems including window wiper motors and even coffee machines.

The culmination of these experiences has led manufacturers to seek suppliers who will engage with them, at the level of the subsystem, in the same style of contracts with which they engage their customers. Without this, vertical integration into design and production activities becomes necessary.

Some balancing is therefore necessary between these two sets of practices. Some design and production capability is needed in the service operations, and some transactional contracts will exist (such as for consumables). How these factors interplay is explored in the following section.

8.3 Impact of Vertical Integration and Organizational Structure

In this section we summarize the rationale underpinning the vertical integration practices of the service operations of manufacturers who are successful in the delivery of advanced services. In summary, these practices are characterized by:

- Extended front-office activities with teams that are aligned around services offerings and coordinated within a matrix-style management structure.

- Retention of some design and production supporting services deployment.

- Relationship-style contracts with some suppliers.

The changes to organizational structure help to alleviate the tensions and trade-offs incurred by delivering differing service offerings. Similarly, the 'relationship'-style contracts are appropriate because

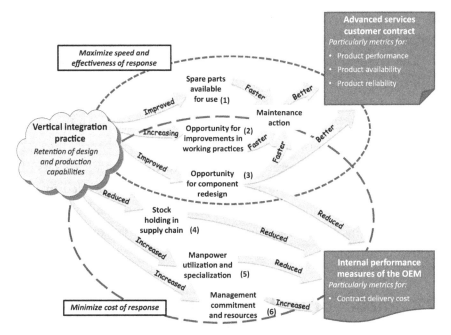

Figure 8.5: *Illustrating the relationship between the vertical integration practice and macro internal performance measures for advanced services*

they align the responsibilities of the supplier with those of the manufacturer. The rationale underpinning the retention of design and production capabilities is more complex. Figure 8.5 illustrates the relationship between these practices and macro internal performance measures.

Retention of design and production capabilities is partially explained by a need to maximize speed and effectiveness of response. For example, if an Alstom train breaks down then reliability penalties will be incurred immediately by the manufacturer (Alstom), and they are closely followed by escalating penalties for lack of availability. Rapid maintenance action is aided by the readiness of spare and replacement parts (item 1 in Figure 8.5). Some commodity parts and consumables (such as hydraulic oils, filters, fasteners and brake components) can be readily held in stock and used on a call-off basis. However, with high-value subsystems, economics demand that these are overhauled and remanufactured.

Retaining design authority also aids continuous improvements in asset design ((2) and (3)). For example, equipment can be readily re-engineered to improve reliability and maintainability (such as improving access to inspection points, lubrication and serviceable items). Likewise, many improvements in working practices (such as those achieved through Lean techniques) have originated from the production environment. Adoption of such techniques in maintenance activities is likely to be assisted if the organization already has expertise of implementing them in production.

Extended design and production capabilities also provide the manufacturer with greater control over the cost of responding. As mentioned above, improvements in working practices and component design impact both the effectiveness and cost of delivering an advanced service. Likewise, the cost of stockholding in the supply chain is reduced (4). Finally, as maintenance operations are notoriously unpredictable, necessitating high levels of buffer capacity in order to deal with unpredictable events, insourcing provides opportunities to better exploit such capacity (5).

An example here is with Alstom on the London Underground Northern Line, where the maintenance depots have chosen to insource the refurbishment of door actuators. This is a relatively low skilled and labour-intensive activity that immediately appears as a candidate for outsourcing if not off-shoring. Yet carrying out such activities internally provides useful employment of maintenance staff during peaks and troughs of service activities, and also helps to reduce stockholding costs of such items.

The downside of this integration is that the business will invariably need to increase investment in management and resources, and this can impact negatively upon the cost of delivering an advanced services contract (6).

8.4 Mitigating the Need for Integration

Holding a set of design and production activities seems an anathema in an age of outsourcing. In the production world, extensive outsourcing and off-shoring have occurred because suppliers are now extremely capable and often in favourable locations for low-cost production. Although advanced services are by their nature more demanding of the manufacturer's responsiveness, questions nevertheless arise around whether this integration is really necessary or is likely to change.

The extent of vertical integration is, however, moderated by a range of factors. Highly significant is the contractual relationship with the suppliers to the manufacturer. Ideally, partners will offer outcome-based contracts that reflect the advanced services offered by the manufacturer. Unfortunately, many suppliers are engaged around product design, manufacture and then sale transaction. Frequently there is too little consideration of their longer-term willingness or ability to support advanced services. Consequently, manufacturers have to extend their vertical integration and stockholding to create a buffer between the relationship services they offer to their customers and the transactional behaviour of their suppliers.

Investments in design and production capabilities are influenced by the available facilities. Facilities that are located close to and distributed throughout customer's operations help to reduce stockholding costs at the sacrifice of manpower and equipment utilization.

Such capabilities are difficult to re-establish once lost to the organization. These underpin the particular advantages that manufacturers hold over more conventional service providers, indeed intellectual property can be generated that can reinforce the manufacturers' own authority over their suppliers. Even when, for example, a subsystem has been sourced from the external supply base the manufacturer can acquire access to intellectual property and develop expertise in the design of equipment for serviceability that can exceed the knowledge of the supplier.

8.5 Chapter Summary

This chapter has dealt with vertical integration issues associated with the delivery of advanced services. In particular it has focused on the internal organizational structure, footprint of operations and relationships with suppliers.

Overall we conclude that the delivery of advanced services requires practices that differ from those we expect in production. Front-office activities are extensive, aligned around differing services offerings, and coordinated by matrix-style management structure. Design and production capabilities are retained to help maximize the speed and effectiveness of response, while helping to minimize costs. Relationships with suppliers move away from transactional contracts.

Instinctively this leads us onto a discussion about business processes. Prior to exploring this, however, we first examine the information and communication technologies around which these processes are commonly crafted.

Chapter 9

INFORMATION AND COMMUNICATION TECHNOLOGIES

E arly on in our programme we quickly recognized that remote product sensing was critically important to the successful delivery of advanced services. As our work progressed, however, we slowly came to appreciate that manufacturers were monitoring much more than simply the condition of their products in the field. Information about location, use, performance, consumption, etc., was all being captured. Frequently this is carried by electronic information and communication technologies (ICTs).

We have captured our principle finding as follows:

> **Principle 4**: Successful delivery of advanced services is enabled by information and communication technologies that are focused on informing and advancing actions of maintenance, repair and use.

In this chapter we examine these technologies. To do this we first look at the overall architecture of a typical ICT system, and then describe each element of the system in turn. We then summarize the rationale that explains why ICTs are so important to the successful delivery of advanced services.

9.1 ICT Architecture in the Delivery of Advanced Services

Information and communication technologies are already widely used in production systems. Manufacturing Resource Planning (MRP II) and Enterprise Resource Planning (ERP) are typical examples of widely used systems. Both are integrated hardware and software applications linked to a central database that stores and delivers business data and information.

MRP II, for example, will facilitate the development of a detailed production schedule based around machine and labour capacity, and scheduling of production runs according to the arrival of materials. Outputs include final labour and machine schedules, along with data about the cost of production, including machine time, labour time and materials used, as well as final production numbers.

Such conventional systems integrate with the operations of both customers and suppliers. In the automotive industry, for instance, they allow first-tier suppliers to link directly with the procurement process of their customers to capture orders for vehicle subassemblies. They then enable these suppliers to place orders on their own supply chain for components and raw materials.

ICTs used in the delivery of advanced services extend this integration. Largely they focus on providing the manufacturer with visibility of their product (or asset) as it is used by the customer. Across our case companies there was a common architecture for such ICT systems. This is illustrated in Figure 9.1.

ICT architecture can be grouped into five functions. *Monitor* is concerned with capturing data from transducers located on critical components or subsystems of the product. *Transmit* deals with the process of communicating either basic data (e.g. temperature, pressure, run time) or fault codes (e.g. overheating, pump failure, scheduled maintenance required) back to the manufacturer. *Store* is concerned

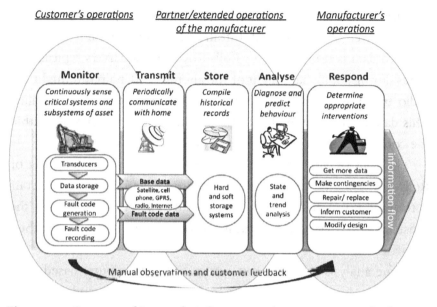

Figure 9.1: *Common architecture for information and communication technologies*

with maintaining records of the transmitted data. *Analyse* deals with the translation of data into information. The *respond* function then establishes any necessary actions that are required (e.g. repair, inform customer, arrange maintenance).

Rolls-Royce provides a helpful illustration of how this process can operate in practice. A gas turbine may, for example, pick up a small foreign object that causes some damage to a compressor blade. Although this is unlikely to have any immediate effect on the engine operation, it can cause a progressive degradation on fuel efficiency and performance.

The Rolls-Royce Engine Health Management (EHM) system has been developed to deal with such eventualities. A microprocessor positioned on the gas turbine constantly monitors around 16 independent parameters (e.g. fuel consumption, vibration, combustion temperature and pressure). A damaged compressor blade will cause a change in such parameters, and the condition monitoring unit will capture this. This may appear initially as a small step change which is then followed by a continued drift in the parameters value.

Such data is transmitted to Rolls-Royce headquarters typically six times during a long haul flight of the aircraft. Older aircraft might use radio transmission, while more recent equipment will use satellite. This data is then channelled to the engineers and technicians within the control centre at Derby in preparation for analysis.

The control centre will be receiving data from the whole fleet of Rolls-Royce engines that are being monitored, and the task of its staff is to trawl through such data, identify any exceptions, tease out the cause, decide how to deal with it, initiate actions and monitor their progress.

Some analysis is carried out automatically. Computer-based algorithms have been developed that look for particular trends amongst the data and compare 'signatures' associated with symptoms of failures. Should matches occur, then 'alert' signals are sent.

In the example of a damaged compressor blade, a change in combustion temperature and pressure is likely to occur. It will be these changes that alert the control centre. If this type of damage is reasonably frequent, then the signature is likely to be well known, and so the particular issue with the engine can be located quickly. Staff will then take a close look at the information and subsequently decide on the corrective action.

Ultimately, this may mean that the aircraft is routed to a maintenance and repair facility for the compressor damage to be rectified. The analysis in the control room may be able to pinpoint the precise subsystem or component that is deteriorating, evaluate the urgency of a repair and ensure that replacement parts are sent to the appropriate repair facility.

With symptoms that occur less frequently, the control room staff may be unable to locate the exact source of the problem with the engine. They may then need additional information which can be gathered by manual observation by a field technician, conversations with the aircraft crew, or feedback from other customer staff. Feedback is also ultimately received from maintenance and repair actions. As each of these failures is dealt with, and records kept, the knowledge base of the manufacturer consequently increases. Hence, their ability to deal with future problems improves.

Manufacturers, however, use ICT for far more than the condition monitoring illustrated by this example. MAN captures information about the way in which the product is used and then use this to modify driver behaviour to improve fuel efficiency. Similarly, Caterpillar dealers monitor location to ensure that their earth-moving machinery is used on the ground that they expect – working in sand can drastically reduce the lifespan of tracks compared to operating in a coalmine.

Finally, these ICT capabilities span the operations of the customer and manufacturer. (*This topic raises various issues that we will discuss in more detail shortly.*) Data capture takes place well within the operations of the customer, whereas in-depth data analysis is usually taken care of within the operations of the manufacturer. The transmission, collection, preliminary data analysis and indeed the techniques for in-depth analysis may be provided by partners of the manufacturer. Companies such as IBM, HCL and Microlise are examples of companies that may partner with manufacturers to provide these capabilities.

In the following section we will delve more deeply into the workings of each of the key functions in the system described in Figure 9.1.

9.2 Monitor

Monitoring is fundamentally concerned with the 'sensing' of critical systems or subsystems of the product (or asset). Deciding which parameters to sense and how to capture data from them is a significant design decision.

Manufacturers choose parameters which reflect the design of the services offering and the role of the product (or asset) in that offering. MAN provides a useful example. Their Trucknology offering targets fuel consumption of trucks by affecting driver behaviour. Critical parameters include the rate of truck acceleration, the extent to which cruise control is used and the harshness of braking. Hence, MAN monitors engine speed and how rapidly this changes.

Such data is, ideally, captured using existing transducers. Much data is readily available from many modern products using existing electronic systems. For instance, the engine management system in MAN vehicles is connected using the vehicle's CANbus to a data acquisition device that allows the continuous collection of information concerning the operation and performance of the vehicle. The engine is permanently fitted with about 25 sensors, many of which are multipurpose.

On some occasions existing sensors are not used, even though they capture key data. Independent systems may also be necessary where there are potential implications to health and safety. For instance, on aircraft gas turbines it is important to isolate the engine management unit (EMU) from the engine health management (EHM) unit.

Additional sensors are also required where existing electronic systems are not present, for example where it is necessary to monitor physical loads and structural integrity. An example of this in practice is on large (300–400 tonne) Caterpillar quarry trucks where an even distribution of spoil is necessary to avoid axel overload. Structural integrity can be assessed by mounting transducers on the parts of the truck's chassis that are known to be at most risk from overload. The positioning of these is critical, and so is informed by finite element analysis during the design. As a consequence such trucks can have as many as 200 sensors fitted.

Advanced services frequently require a wide portfolio of additional data. Location, for example, is often important and can be provided by GPS. Some Caterpillar dealers will limit their lease agreements to particular locations, and so will expect their equipment to operate within a small area associated with that location. Similarly, knowing where equipment is located is helpful when arranging to carry out maintenance activities – especially when many machines are operating on the same site.

Once data is captured it can be analysed locally or remotely. It is now quite common for the data to be fed into a localized microprocessor which will carry out some analysis and generate fault codes. These are then stored locally, and can be accessed by technicians at periodic maintenance intervals. Advanced services, however, require data to be transmitted from the asset back to the manufacturer.

9.3 Transmit and Store

Two forms of data are commonly transmitted. Sometimes simply 'base data' from transducers is transmitted (e.g. engine temperature, oil pressure, location). In other cases, the fault codes arising from the on-board microprocessor are transmitted. Both approaches are widely used.

Rolls-Royce Gas Turbines tend to transmit mainly base data from a relatively small set of sensors (approximately 16). Most modern large civil aircraft use satellite communication. Two types of transmissions usually take place. Regular reports are made during take-off, climb and once the aircraft is in cruise. These are snapshots of performance. Special reports are also triggered by unusual engine conditions. A worldwide ground network then transfers this data to the intended destination.

Alstom trains, by contrast, transmit fault codes from a wide array of on-board subsystems, for example an on-board train management system (TMS) that monitors a range of 25 train systems including propulsion, tilt, high tension, braking, air, etc., using some 15 computers interfaced to various on-board sensors. This data is transmitted electronically via track-side data collection units.

Data can be transmitted in a variety of ways. Radio and satellite are common, so too are the internet and dedicated hard-wired systems. Xerox, for instance, use internet links for their printing systems.

9.4 Analyse and Respond

As soon as the individual reports arrive at the manufacturer they are processed automatically. The data is checked for validity and corrections applied to normalize them. Analysis can then be thought of in terms of diagnostics and prognostics. Typical techniques use signal analysis to identify the current and likely future 'health' of an asset.

Automated algorithms can be used to do this, and the results cross-checked with multiple sensor information to provide a sensitive detection capability. Manual oversight is still an important part of the process, because false alerts can cause unnecessary maintenance actions to be taken.

As in the medical world, expert knowledge is then used to turn a symptom into a diagnosis and usually a prognosis. This is done by using the skills of engineers to assess the most likely physical cause of a particular fault signature, how an operator can confirm this, and how urgently this needs to be carried out.

The technical helpdesk will discuss the recommendations with the operator (to manage the best fit with their planned operation) and will then liaise regularly with them until the problem is understood and any risk to the smooth operation of their service mitigated.

Sophisticated product-centric service and support contracts are frequently coupled with the OEM undertaking greater risk exposure and so the asset (product) in question is designed to be capable of being 'interrogated' locally and/or remotely.

Manual observation and customer feedback also form part of the information set at the control centre. This information set is used to generate advanced warning of potential problems and enables the scheduling of materials and/or resources to undertake any necessary maintenance/repair activities, implement contingency actions, inform the customer and also feed back to the product design process if needed.

Manual observation also occurs in practice in, for instance, situations where reassurance is needed about the overall use of products. Caterpillar dealers may assign a technician to watch over their equipment in large quarrying operations and cross check with data arising from ICTs on how well quarry trucks are being driven. Some parameters are difficult to monitor using ICT; the condition of paintwork on leased cars is an example of where checks need to be performed by staff.

Remote monitoring can also be carried out without ICTs. Oil sampling is one example of this. Samples of lubrication oil can be taken periodically from equipment and then analysed in a laboratory. Here, the presence of metals such as phosphor-bronze might indicate bearing wear, whereas fuel contamination and water can suggest poor combustion or leaking systems.

Although such monitoring is not in real-time, it is nevertheless valuable within well-established processes. So too is the assessment of equipment during routine maintenance and repair. A popular practice on large diesel engines is the use of a simple magnetic sump plug that can give advanced warning of wear during oil changes. Likewise, the close examination of components during repair and overhaul can indicate how products have been used in the field.

9.5 Impact of ICT Capabilities

ICT systems provide visibility of the product (or asset) as it is used by the customer. The relationship between the enabling ICT and business pressures is captured in Figure 9.2. This illustrates the various ways in which such capabilities support the manufacturer in the delivery of advanced services.

The enabling technology and systems practices provide better visibility of the asset in use in terms of condition, operating characteristics, time in use and location. The remote access to this information for the service provider facilitates more timely awareness of faults to provide faster maintenance/repair actions and can lead to improved equipment design, operator behaviour and less need for manual obser-

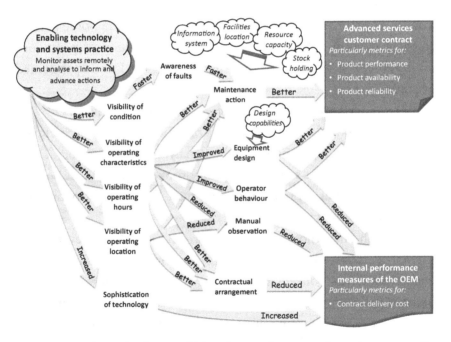

Figure 9.2: *Relationship between ICT and internal-macro performance measures for advanced services*

vation of the asset in the field. The resulting improved responsiveness of the service provider has a positive impact on asset performance and availability, while the improvements in design and operator behaviour have a positive impact on reliability.

The increasing sophistication of enabling technologies and systems has a downside in that it contributes to an increase in service delivery costs. However, the visibility of asset operating characteristics, time in use and location provided can help to mitigate some of the risks adopted by the service provider and relieve contract delivery costs. Improvements in product reliability and availability can also reduce both service delivery cost and the need for manual observation/ intervention within the delivery system.

These enabling technology and systems practices, and their impact on business performance, are moderated by other practices within the broader service delivery system. Key here is design and technical capabilities together with integrated information systems. As illustrated in Figure 9.2, decisions about these other practices impact the consequences of the technology and systems practices in a number of ways. For example, design and technical capability and resources are essential to an effective problem response process, as is the ability to integrate information systems to plan materials and resources in a timely and accurate manner.

9.6 Chapter Summary

The integration of technology with supporting management processes is fundamental to the primary value proposition of cost-effective delivery of service. Realizing the benefits from the application of such enabling technology is dependent on the effective integration of operations management, control management and maintenance management. However, cohesion of these functions can be dependent on multiple stakeholder input with potentially conflicting interests. Achieving the required changes can present a significant organizational challenge to companies delivering product-centric services through the use of enabling technologies.

The application of emerging technology is improving the performance of the service delivery supply chain. In the case of high-value capital assets, management of the supply chain will benefit from further research into technologies that enable more accurate through-life costing, the provision of through-life engineering services and self-healing technologies for electronic and mechanical components and subsystems.

Chapter 10

The evolution of the manufacturing industry has seen significant changes in the organization and skill-sets of workers. During the industrial revolution of the 1700s, for example, the introduction of the assembly line meant that relatively unskilled men and women (who were trained to carry out small repetitive tasks) could significantly increase their output over artisans in the conventional craft-based systems. Henry Ford is well known for using such systems to revolutionize automotive manufacture, and these have endured within mass production. Toyota still uses many aspects of the moving assembly line first pioneered by Ford.

The process of servitization also demands innovations in the way people are organized and skilled, their culture and how they are led and incentivized. We have examined this topic partially in section 8.2, where we described how successfully servitized manufacturers create an extended front office for their people involved in delivering advanced services. In this chapter we look within this front office to examine the desired behaviour of the workers. In particular we question *who are the staff that are located in such an office; how do they behave; and what skill-sets are necessary for them to be successful in the delivery of advanced services?*

Our focus is largely on skill-sets. Ultimately it is the 'behaviour' of the people in the front office that is most important. We know that behaviour is affected by an array of factors; physical condition (i.e. age, gender, strength, dexterity), psychological attributes (i.e. personality, attitudes, beliefs, emotions), work environment (i.e. heat, light, noise, vibration) and the social environment (i.e. leadership, team working, communication, motivation and reward structures). Yet, in practice, only a few of these factors can be modified by the manufacturer.

Skill-sets can be identified and developed. Some people have an aptitude for particular skills and so are more easily nurtured; others have an aversion and so are limited in the role they can take in service delivery. Recruitment processes can test for skills, worker selection can be carried out, and developmental training can be given. These processes are enabled by our knowledge of those skill-sets that are important.

To identify these skill-sets we first identified and examined the various roles of front-office workers. We then established the desirable behaviours associated with each role, and then amalgamated our findings into a set of six important behaviours. We only sought behaviours that were distinctive to the delivery of advanced services, and dismissed those 'hygiene' factors which are desirable in all workers (i.e. an ability to start work on time and work safely). Finally, we identified those skill-sets that were most supportive of these distinctive behaviours, and captured these in the following principle that we explain in this section:

> **Principle 5**: Successful delivery of advanced services is enabled by staff, who are co-located in a front office and skilled in being flexible, relationship builders, service-centric, authentic, technically adept and resilient.

This chapter will explain this practice, why it is favoured, and summarize the factors that mitigate the impact.

10.1 Deployment of Staff in the Delivery of Advanced Services

With advanced services much more of the manufacturer's organization comes into contact with the customer. In section 8.2 we introduced the idea of a front office, and that this refers to those departments that come into direct contact with customers. With advanced services these operations are also much more extensive than those in a production setting, as the manufacturer carries out a range of activities which would otherwise be performed by the customer themselves (e.g. project management, maintenance, repair, condition monitoring).

We also introduced the term 'back office'. We use this to refer to those production-centred activities that are usually associated with product manufacture (e.g. product design, development, production). We also stress that the front-office/back-office distinction is defined by the nature and focus of activities, and should not be confused with the physical location of facilities. *But what of the people who work within the front office?* On close inspection the front office of manufacturers delivering advanced services is split. Some staff are 'frontline' while others are 'support' (Table 10.1).

Frontline staff interface directly with the customer. Staff here include project managers, account managers and field engineers. Typically, frontline staff will interact with (or touch) customers perhaps weekly; indeed in some instances staff might be co-located in a control room which is within the customer's facilities and so meet daily. These might be customer staff who are responsible for managing contracts, or staff who are monitoring closely the operation of equipment.

Table 10.1 Deployment of staff in the delivery of advanced services

Categories	Deployment	
	Front office	Back office
Overall focus of staff	Delivery of product–service offerings	Product design and manufacture
Typical role of staff	Frontline customer contact	Support customer contact	Enable customer contact through product manufacture
Examples of staff in role	Account sales/managers, contract sales, field engineers, operations centre manager, customer services agreement manager	Condition-monitoring technicians, technical services manager, general managers of parts and service, product support manager	Research scientists, engineering design, production management, production engineering
Usual contact person within customer	Project manager, account manager, equipment operative	Equipment operative	Equipment operatives, project managers, account managers
Extent and frequency of customer interaction	High/maybe daily or hourly	Medium/maybe weekly	Low/periodically and arranged around new product introduction/factory inspections and tours

Field engineers are a good example of typical frontline staff. These engineers have frequent and extended interactions with the customer, especially equipment operatives. So influential are these interactions that in some cases field engineers are scheduled always to arrive at customers facilities (say for scheduled maintenance activities) just prior to equipment being shut down (rather than after). In this way the engineer can meet the operatives, and so sustain relationships with customer personnel, as well as gain insight into any early signs of equipment failure that might go undetected by other condition monitoring systems.

Support staff assist those in the frontline. Staff in these roles include parts and services managers, condition monitoring technicians and workshop managers. They tend to interact directly with these rather than the customers and are only likely to discuss with the customer's own staff when, for example, diagnosing an equipment fault. Indeed, these support staff may have skills more usually associated with the back office.

A condition monitoring technician is a good example of a support staff member. These staff will typically be located in a control centre where they can remotely monitor information about the condition, use and performance of products. Should any anomalies arise, they will then work to address these through field engineers, project managers and other frontline staff.

10.2 Behaviour and Skill-Sets of Front-Office Staff

People in services behave differently than those in production. Just about all of the managers we interviewed indicated that gaining the right behaviour from staff to achieve a 'services culture' was a significant challenge. To achieve this there is a set of six 'humanistic' behaviours that are important (Figure 10.1).

Figure 10.1: *Behaviours of the archetypal front-office worker*

Overall they behave as an advocate for the customer, they develop meaningful relationships with the customer, they understand the customer's business, and they know what causes 'pain' to the customer. They also develop strong relationships with people in their own internal organization and sacrifice their own schedules and commitments to help address customer issues.

Front-office staff are also technically capable; they understand the technologies and systems that form their offering to the customer, and are realistic when making commitments around these. Yet they are also robust. They recognize that both the customer and manufacturer have imperfections that are beyond their control, and when these are enacted, they don't see these as a failing of themselves.

Some of this humanistic behaviour is attributable to a person's natural tendency to be outgoing and socially engaging. Yet there are six skills which, as an integrated skill-set, underpin these archetypal behaviours. These are summarized in Table 10.2. Here, we take the term skill to refer to an ability to do something well, often gained through training and/or experience.

Table 10.2 Humanistic principal skill-sets expected of front-office staff

Desired behaviour	Supportive skills	Description of skills
Readily have meaningful conversations with customers Forging strong people/team relationships with other staff within the front office	Relationship building	Ability to develop and sustain close customer trust, and similar relationships with other staff internal to the manufacturer
Prepared to vary working hours or task to match customer demand	Flexible	Ability to modify working routine in order to comply with customer requirements
Appreciating the consequences of an equipment failure on the customers of our customer Talking to people, engaging people and understanding where they are coming from	Service-centric	An empathy with customer's problems and delivering against these; capable of putting themselves in the customer's shoes
Demonstrating belief in the manufacturer, its products and services Only making commitments that can be fully delivered	Authentic	Genuinely committed to delivering a successful outcome for the customer; prepared to tell the customer the truth
Being able to understand the consequences of an electrical subsystem failure on a machine	Technically adept	Understanding of the principal operation and subsystems of products and equipment
Appreciating when the customer's anxiety is with the situation although it may come across as more personal: being able to sleep at night!	Resilient	Capable of dealing with the personal stress incurred by working at the frontline with the customer

Relationship building

Relationship building is a skill in initiating, developing and sustaining communication and interactions with others. This skill enables meaningful and relevant conversations with customers, and engenders support from other service staff. People who are skilful are good at making connections and recognize that even strong relationships can be irreparably damaged by a few moments of careless comments and/ or actions.

This skill is strongly linked to 'resilience' which we will discuss in a moment. In the delivery of advanced services, it is those relationships formed in the 'heat of the battle' rather than on the golf course which are most valued. People with this skill are highly prized.

Flexible

As a skill, flexibility refers to an ability to modify working routine in order to comply with customer requirements and yet remain effective. Some people are most comfortable and effective when they work within structured routines. The classical factory typifies this with its shift-systems for the shop floor and 9 am–5 pm working day for office workers. Services are different and demand people who are capable of working varying hours or tasks to match customer demand.

An illustration of this skill being enacted is given by the example of unscheduled maintenance work on trains. Take the situation where should a train breakdown and not be available for use then significant financial penalties are levied on the manufacturer for every minute of unavailability. Because such breakdowns are difficult to predict, the manufacturer has to be able arrange maintenance staff as required. This unpredictability coupled with penalties gives a dilemma. *Should expensive maintenance staff be kept, on stand-by, within the repair facility just in case? If so, how many? Where should they be located? What should they be doing while waiting for a failure?*

Two solutions are enabled by people with a skill in working flexibly. Maintenance crews on the London Underground Northern Line are kept on stand-by at the depot, but when they are not required, they engage in the overhaul of relatively low-tech equipment. For example, they may replace the rubber seals on pneumatic door actuators, a task that can be picked up and put down at a moment's notice. An alternative is to allow maintenance crews to be at home but on-call. The understanding being that should a failure occur then they have to respond immediately. This is not necessarily an 'overtime' arrangement, but rather part of an 'annualized hours agreement'.

Service-centric

Service-centricity is closely coupled to both relationship building and flexibility, and refers to a skill of being able to empathize with a customer's situation. In other words, a skill in seeing a problem through the eyes of the customer, and appreciating the consequences of an equipment failure on the customer's business.

Advanced service contracts demand and reward a skill in service-centricity. In our earlier discussion of performance measures (section 6.1) we highlighted that the principal measures are 'those of the customer'. All others cascade from these. Measures such as 'lost passenger hours' (in the case of the London Underground Northern Line) mean that advanced services are inherently customer focused. This also means that any failure to deliver these by the manufacturer directly hurts the customer's business.

Staff who are skilled in service-centricity understand this situation and modify their behaviour to reflect this. For example, they understand that should a train fail to leave a station on time, or a quarry truck fail on the haul road of a mine, their customers' business will be affected. They will then respond to this, and take actions that may readily exceed their contracted obligations. For the manufacturer, a pay-back is that when a customer sees such behaviour they can be more relaxed about executing penalties.

In our study we found many instances where manufacturers recruited staff from their own customers so that they could improve their capacity to empathize. For instance, we came across senior people within services at Rolls-Royce who had been recruited from customers such as Cathy Pacific and Singapore Airlines. The motive was simply to improve capacity within Rolls-Royce services staff to 'think like the customer'.

Authentic

Authenticity refers to the extent to which the staff are able to be genuine, open and honest with the customer. This is not to suggest that some people willingly mislead a customer, but rather that openly telling the truth about the extent of a situation can be extremely uncomfortable. As we mentioned earlier, advanced services are a high-pressure situation where failure of the manufacturer can directly hurt the performance and reputation of its customer. All staff can understandably become stressed and anxious.

Those who are skilled in being authentic will be bold and explain difficult situations to their customers. Perhaps this is eased when other skills interplay; strong relationships and service-centricity help elevate the severity of the situation. A second aspect of this skill is a demonstrable belief in the manufacturer and its products and services. Ultimately they will only make commitments that can be fully delivered.

Technically adept

Technically adept means being skilled in understanding the operation of a machine, subsystem and the application. Ultimately, this skill means that the frontline staff are credible to both the customer and their own support team.

Our work with Caterpillar dealers provides a helpful illustration. Their ICT capabilities gave reports on the distance equipment had travelled during a working day. When we first observed such data we thought that this might generally help with calculating wear and tear. Yet the condition-monitoring staff saw much more immediate significance in, for example, a quarry truck travelling 40 miles per day and a tracked excavator traversing less than half a mile. Their concern would be with the excavator as these machines are designed to be operated over a very small area. They might then contact both the customer to understand the reason for the action and, should it happen regularly, alert field engineers about possible maintenance issues.

Resilient

Resilience refers to an ability to deal with and recover quickly from setbacks – for instance, dealing with the stress incurred by working at the frontline with the customer, and appreciating when the customer's anxiety is with the situation even though it may come across as more personal. Ultimately, the measure of this skill is an ability to sleep at night!

10.3 Culture, Leadership and Incentives in the Front Office

So far our focus has been on skill-sets as, relative to other factors, these can be readily identified and developed. Yet we also recognize that other factors in the front office can moderate the behaviour of staff. In particular the social environment in terms of culture, leadership and motivations. Here, we must again emphasize that we are only concerned with those aspects that affect the successful delivery of advanced services. Across our cases culture, leadership and incentives were such factors.

Culture

Culture generally refers to the atmosphere within an organization, and can be defined as:

- An integrated pattern of human knowledge, belief and behaviour that depends upon the capacity for symbolic thought and social learning.

- The set of shared attitudes, values, goals and practices that characterizes an institution, organization or group.

It is essential to create a fair and cooperative culture in the front office, along with mutually consistent goals among the staff, and a shared interest in being successful. Various techniques were evident in our case companies for achieving such goals. In Alstom, for instance, there were very clear 'rules of the depot' which set out the values and processes of the front office.

Behaviour was also sustained by a comparable balance of power across the front/back offices, and here there appears to be bias towards the office which is the principal source of revenue. Evidence was apparent of front-office staff taking senior positions within the host manufacturer, and this was to ensure all operations are orientated towards customer service.

This helped to ensure that the culture was consistent with the expectations and working of the front office and an acceptance that these may be different to production. For example, managers in the front office may be more willing to accept the difficulty of attaining the same high levels of worker and machine utilization than would normally be achieved within production.

Leadership

Sustaining the desired behaviour of front-office staff generates particular demands of leadership. Leadership style refers to a leader's behaviour; different situations call for different leadership styles. In an emergency, when there is little time to converge on an agreement and where a designated authority has significantly more experience or expertise than the rest of the team, an autocratic leadership style may be most effective. However, in a highly motivated and aligned team with a homogeneous level of expertise, a more democratic or laissez-faire style may be more effective. The style adopted should be the one that most effectively achieves the objectives of the group while balancing the interests of its individual members.

Incentives

An incentive is any factor (financial or non-financial) that enables or motivates a particular course of action, or counts as a reason for preferring one choice to the alternatives. It is an expectation that encourages people to behave in a certain way. Ultimately, incentives aim to provide value for money and contribute to organizational success.

Incentive structures, however, are notoriously trickier than they might appear to people who set them up. Human beings are both finite and creative; that means that the people offering incentives are often unable to predict all of the ways that people will respond to them. Thus, imperfect knowledge and unintended consequences can often make incentives much more complex than the people offering them originally expected, and can lead either to unexpected windfalls or to disasters produced by unintentionally perverse incentives.

10.4 Impact of an Integrated Skill-Set

The six skills collectively represent a skill-set. Invariably some people in the front office will be more developed in these than others, and this will be reflected in their roles. For example, although they can both be thought of as front-office staff, a condition-monitoring technician will need stronger technical skills relative to an account sales manager, who will correspondingly need to be stronger at relationship building. Yet to a greater or lesser extent all staff in the front office will be expected to possess and apply all the skills.

Even when a person is skilled in all these there will still be broader trade-offs. For example, back-office staff such as designers are likely to have stronger technical skills. Therefore, front-office staff will be expected to link to these when needed. For instance, if an aircraft is damaged in use then specialist analysis may need to be undertaken by airworthiness engineers to establish the appropriate repairs. Such safety critical analysis would be undertaken by back-office staff, with the technical support team of the front office providing the necessary field data and customer interactions.

In this way the back office is shielded from direct interactions with the customer. The reason for this was succinctly captured by the parts and services manager in one of our cases, who commented that *'manufacturing people rarely understand service'*. In this way the technical support staff in the front office become brokers for finding solutions to problems.

The skill-sets summarized in Table 10.2 exist because they are considered by our case companies to be key to the successful delivery of advanced services. They also gave the rationale that explains how these support the attainment of key performance measures for advanced services contracts. As before, these are measures of asset performance, availability and reliability, which need to be delivered at the lowest cost.

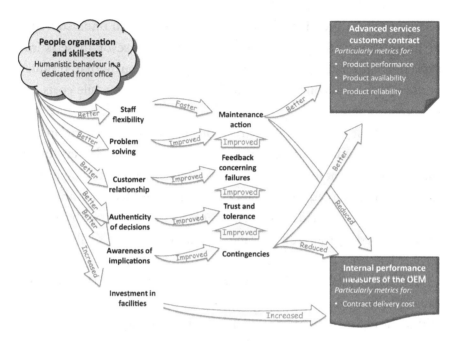

Figure 10.2: *Relationship between humanistic behaviour and internal-macro perform-ance measures for advanced services*

Figure 10.2 illustrates this general relationship as an influence diagram, showing how the practice in people organization and skill-sets translates into successful delivery of an advanced services contract. Here, we have summarized the practices as humanistic behaviour in a dedicated front office.

These practices require considerable investment from the host manufacturer. Concentrating resources in this way requires dedicated facilities, with people whose skills and training differ from those in production. We have shown in Figure 10.2 how this will adversely affect the cost of delivering advanced services.

By contrast the deployment and skill-sets of people, as we have described in this chapter, will deliver distinct advantages. In particular capabilities in terms of staff flexibility, problem solving, customer relationships, authenticity of decision making, and an understanding of implications of actions. The overall consequence of these is improved maintenance actions and contingencies, such that product performance, availability and reliability are enhanced, while costs are kept to a minimum.

An example of this complete relationship in action occurred in one of our case studies. The company concerned provided a customer support agreement for maintenance on aircraft. The contract specified that any unscheduled maintenance should be performed within two days. The company had an incident where an issue arose with avionics which caused the aircraft to land prematurely in a small regional airport late on a Friday evening.

The airport had very limited maintenance facilities. This incident caused an immediate alert within the front-office control centre. Staff within the centre had sufficient technical skills to diagnose the problem and identify a solution without having to call on the design specialists within the manufacturer. Unfortunately, the lack of facilities meant that repairs would take longer than usual and compromise the availability measure.

The front-office staff then communicated and discussed the problem and solution with the customer and, because of the strength and credibility of the relationship, the customer was prepared to adjust its flight schedules to accommodate the unavailable aircraft. A repair crew travelled simultaneously to the regional airport and worked on the aircraft over the weekend to get it operational as quickly as possible.

The aircraft was repaired and was operational by the following Monday and, although this exceeded the window for unscheduled availability, because the contingencies of the manufacturer worked well the airline company chose to forgo any penalty claims they may have otherwise made.

10.5 Chapter Summary

This chapter has dealt with the deployment and skill-sets of people with whom our successful companies engage to deliver advanced services. In summary this is enabled by staff, who are co-located in a front office and skilled in being flexible, relationship builders, service-centric, authentic, technically adept and resilient. These skill sets differ significantly to those valued in production. While the location and deployment of these staff are critical, so too are the business processes that orchestrate their actions. This is the topic of the next chapter.

Chapter 11

Business processes are frequently overlooked during debates about advanced services. Rarely will academics or practitioners engage with this topic with the same enthusiasm as they show for new information and communication technologies. Yet such processes are the threads that pull together the information, people and facilities that are essential in the support of advanced services.

The relationships that these processes engender between the customer and manufacturer are given more attention. Yet these are often misunderstood and treated as a component of the service offering to the customer. In practice, a move away from a transactional approach to doing business, to one where there are strong relationships in place throughout the life-cycle of the service offering, is an important aspect of the service delivery system itself. Advanced services are enabled by strong relationships between the customer and manufacturer, and these relationships are fostered by people and the processes that guide their behaviour.

We have captured this situation with processes and relationships as:

> **Principle 6**: Success with servitization is enabled by organizational processes that are integrated into a wide range of customer 'touch-points', fostering strong inter-organizational relationships at these, to manage proactively the condition, use and location of assets in the field.

In this chapter we explore this topic in detail, and begin by briefly reflecting on the form that processes and relationships take in a production-centric environment.

11.1 Services Processes in a Production Environment

Our concern is with those business processes that formalize the interactions between the manufacturer and their customers. In particular, the form these processes take to successfully deliver advanced services. A helpful starting point is to reflect on how these are characterized in a production environment.

Figure 11.1 illustrates a typical situation. Three sets of largely independent interactions or 'touch-points' occur between the manufacturer and customer.

Product sale incurs various negotiations between the customer and manufacturer which, if successful, lead to the delivery of the product into the field. For the manufacturer, the outcomes from these interactions are 'demand signals' for new product design and manufacture. While for the customer, these can be thought of as a series of 'experiences' that extend through the life-cycle of the product.

A large portion of this life-cycle is the 'use' phase. The customer operates the product and in doing so gains experiences of the performance. By contrast, this is rarely a touch-point with the manufacturer.

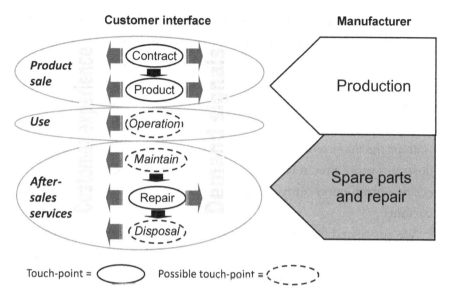

Figure 11.1: *Interactions between the manufacturer and customer in a typical production context*

Interactions with the customers tend to be indirect, with the manufacturer having to rely on customer surveys and the conversations of sales staff to gain feedback.

This situation changes with after-sales services. Typically these are instigated should the product fail or begin to degrade. The customer is likely to be the first to know about such issues; a truck may fail to start, or hydraulic oil leaks may appear on the excavator's actuators. Often faults are picked up during routine maintenance, which the customer may well carry out themselves.

The manufacturer may only become engaged to provide services that rectify the fault. Linked into after-sales services is the disposal of the product at its end-of-life. The manufacturer may be involved in this, or the customer may take care of disposal themselves.

After-sales services provide the customer with a range of experiences. Yet for the manufacturer visibility of the product is limited to just a few touch-points that create demand signals for spare parts and repairs. Even these are dependent on the manufacturer having been successful in winning the after-sales services, rather than these being performed either by the customer themselves or an independent services provider.

These after-sales services are base and intermediate services. *So what are the characteristics of the business processes seen here?* Figure 11.2 illustrates more precisely what occurs in archetypical after-sales services in a production-centric environment when a product fails out of warranty.

We suggested above that the customer is likely to be the first to recognize that a product is degrading or has failed. Exceptions occur, for example, when the manufacturer is engaged to perform scheduled maintenance or certification and in doing so registers a fault. Or, the product may already be in repair with the manufacturer when additional faults are found.

Once a fault is found, this invariably instigates a negotiation process between the customer and manufacturer. The extent, price and dead-

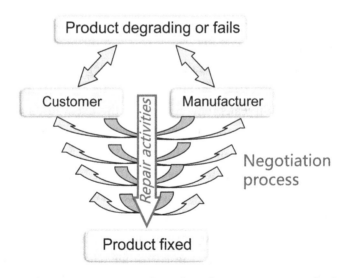

Figure 11.2: *Reactive process typical to after-sales services in a production-centric environment*

lines for the repair will be debated. This debate might extend into warranty claims, and so responsibilities for the repair, and even possibilities for product replacement. The more complex and expensive the repair, the more convoluted this negotiation process. During this time the asset is invariably out of use.

Once a repair is commissioned this negotiation process may well continue. Repairs are often carried out on the basis of 'time and materials' consumed, and on expensive repairs the customer may be required to make staged payments for the work. All this time the customer becomes anxious about costs, often perceiving progress as creeping along, while their own revenue generation on the equipment effectively stops.

The perceptions of the customer are understandable, but their urgency is not necessarily reflected in the processes of the manufacturer's repair facilities. Internally, the manufacturer may manage their people and facilities to gain resource efficiencies, choosing to schedule and prioritize activities to maximize resource utilization. Should, for example, a repair be waiting upon the arrival of spare parts, then workers will be moved to another task until these arrive. Larger customers are often given preferential treatment, even though their needs might not warrant prioritization.

Eventually a crisis point can occur. The customer becomes so anxious that they complain to senior management. In response, staff within the repair facility change their priorities. Often, a staff member will take on the role of a 'white knight', taking personal responsibility for progress – reprioritizing and scheduling activities to expedite the customer's repair.

The system reacts following a process that can best be described as 'heroic recovery' – during which time other customers perceive progress on their repairs to be slow, and so this 'reactive' cycle begins again.

Such processes foster 'transactional' interactions between the staff of the customer and those of the manufacturer. For example, when the manufacturer has an opportunity to inspect the product or equipment it is in their own interest to identify as many faults as possible and to stress their severity. By contrast, the customer will seek to ignore all but the critical issues and, where possible, place some of the blame for these back on the design and production of the product, and then seek recompense from the manufacturer for these. Either way, once the repair is made, the transaction is complete, and the process ends.

11.2 Business Processes in the Delivery of Advanced Services

In the production world, those business processes that deal with after-sales services are characteristically 'reactive'. They are designed to respond to the customer orders for spare parts, repairs or overhaul, and often incur a raft of interactions and negotiation within the fulfilment process.

The processes with advanced services are different. Fundamentally, this is because advanced services focus on providing 'capability' as an outcome rather than simply maintenance of a product's condition. Coupled to this are extended life-cycles of the offering, over which time the manufacturer has increased responsibilities, and in return for fulfilling these receives relatively linear revenue flow (sections 3.4 and 3.5).

Consequently the processes have more extensive customer touch-points; these are interconnected, and send many more demand signals to the manufacturer for which there are clear incentives to respond. Figure 11.3 illustrates the situation.

Advanced services extend the manufacturer's operations into those of the customer (section 8.2). This change in organizational positioning means that there are now many more points of contact with the

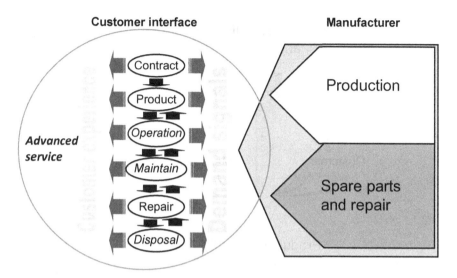

Figure 11.3: *Interactions between the manufacturer and customer in an advanced service*

customer. For instance, MAN trucks, Northern Line Trains, and Rolls-Royce Gas Turbines are monitored during their operation using the ICT capabilities we presented in the previous chapter. Similarly, there are many more opportunities for the manufacturer's front-office staff to interact with the customer, whether this be engineers maintaining products in the field, or project managers scheduling maintenance with the customer's staff.

Additionally, these touch-points are interconnected to reflect the life-cycle of an advanced service contract (Figure 3.4). Once a contract is in place, product selection, operation, maintenance, repair and even disposal are integrated to provide the customer with the desired 'capability'. Collectively these provide a complete customer experience.

The demand signals on the manufacturer also have to be treated collectively. This is because advanced services are themselves coupled with the manufacturer taking responsibility should the customer experience be substandard. Customer facing measures are in place

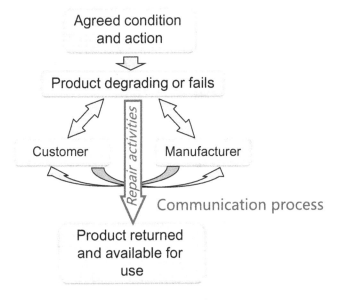

Figure 11.4: *Proactive process typical to advanced services*

to capture this whole experience, such as 'lost passenger hours' (section 6.1).

Any failure to respond to a demand signal may very well result in penalties being levied on the manufacturer. Consequently, the manufacturer is now incentivized to have in place processes that enable them to respond urgently should any issues occur with their product. The result is the process characteristics represented in Figure 11.4.

Structurally the processes used in the successful delivery of advanced services differ significantly to those in the production-centric environment. Rather than reacting to a product failure, through a negotiation process to arrive at a repair activity, these processes are proactive in character.

At the outset of the contract, policies are established which agree the condition of the product and the actions necessary to maintain this. For example, a Caterpillar quarry truck might have an agreed 'availability' of 20 hours each day, on the understanding that for the remaining four hours the truck is given over to the Caterpillar dealer for scheduled maintenance and minor repairs.

The interactions between the customer and manufacturer are then around communication rather that negotiating an action. For example, should the quarry truck become available earlier, the manufacturer will be informed so that they can use any extra time to execute more lengthy repairs. Alternatively, the manufacturer might on occasion struggle with a repair, meaning that the truck is unavailable. Here, the customer will be informed so that contingencies can be executed.

The outcome of the whole process is that the product is returned to be available for use rather than simply repaired. The manufacturer is incentivized to achieve this by penalties associated with the customer facing performance measures (section 6.1). So, in the example above, where the truck is not available for use, the manufacturer will be penalized.

Yet across the companies we have studied, both the customer and the manufacturer seek to avoid penalty payments. The behaviour of the customer is initially surprising. The reasoning is that the customers of these advanced services contracts recognize that their revenue is generated through the use of the product and not through penalizing the manufacturer. For instance, the priority of train operators such as Virgin is to avoid customer disruption, rather than accept disruptions simply because they allow a clawback of revenues from Alstom.

As a consequence, we have seen that customers are actually quite tolerant of manufacturers, and will be somewhat relaxed in their use of penalties if the manufacturer is seen to be passionate and investing heavily to fulfil customer facing measures. Yet penalty systems will be invoked aggressively if this is not the case.

This communication process extends across all partners in the delivery process. This allows the communication and management of failures to the whole system. Overall these processes are not, however, heavily formalized and documented. During our study we found that manufacturers would willingly provide schematics that illustrated the general process structure. These would be sufficient to communicate the general architecture of the system and key decision points, but rarely did these go into overwhelming detail.

This is not to suggest that these companies are failing, but rather it reflects the extent of uncertainties with advanced services. Where possible processes are documented in depth, for example how to respond to a fault code being received from a truck engine. Underpinning these, however, is a reliance on the skill-sets of the service staff who are in the frontline of supporting the contract.

11.3 Proactive Processes as the Core for Advanced Services Delivery

Previous chapters have introduced a raft of technologies and practices that are key to the successful delivery of advanced services, explaining how these differ to what would be found in a production-centric environment. For each we have provided an influence diagram that illustrates the relationship between the practice and delivery of an advanced service (e.g. Figure 9.2). We were also able to explain how this relationship is mitigated by practices in other areas. For example, the need for staff to be co-located within a customer's operations can be relaxed by ICT systems with strong prognostic capabilities (providing advanced warning of an impending product failure and so greater time for people to react). This is not the case with proactive processes.

Processes are at the core of advanced services delivery. They integrate the performance measurement systems, facilities, organizational structure, technology systems and people. Figure 11.5 illustrates how these elements are integrated through the contract delivery process.

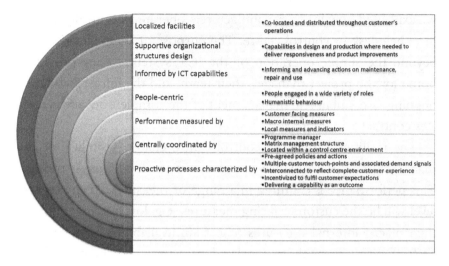

Localized facilities	•Co-located and distributed throughout customer's operations
Supportive organizational structures design	•Capabilities in design and production where needed to deliver responsiveness and product improvements
Informed by ICT capabilities	•Informing and advancing actions on maintenance, repair and use
People-centric	•People engaged in a wide variety of roles •Humanistic behaviour
Performance measured by	•Customer facing measures •Macro internal measures •Local measures and indicators
Centrally coordinated by	•Programme manager •Matrix management structure •Located within a control centre environment
Proactive processes characterized by	•Pre-agreed policies and actions •Multiple customer touch-points and associated demand signals •Interconnected to reflect complete customer experience •Incentivized to fulfil customer expectations •Delivering a capability as an outcome

Figure 11.5: *Illustrating how processes are core to integrated technologies and practices in advanced services delivery*

Underpinning this whole integration are the characteristics of the processes themselves. These are proactive and characterized by the features we described above, such as pre-agreed policies and action, and strong incentives for the manufacturer to fulfil the customer's expectations. In practice there are a plethora of processes and sub-processes needed to fulfil an advanced services contract.

Ultimately these processes are owned and coordinated from a central control point. Across the cases we studied, there was always a project/programme manager who held overall responsibility for these processes. Frequently they operated in a matrix management structure which allowed them to cut across functions and exercise authority for complete contract fulfilment. The project manager may have frequent interactions with the customer, and is often thought of as the advocate for the contract within the manufacturer's organization.

The project manager (and team) is almost always centrally located in a control centre. This centralized facility is at the heart of the contract fulfilment process. Earlier, in our description of ICT capabilities, we explained how leading manufacturers operated a centralized technical helpdesk or control centre. The purpose of these facilities goes beyond the simple operation of the ICT systems. They provide a home for the project manager, their team, and the infrastructure for ongoing assessment and management of the complete advanced services contract.

The facilities within the control centre enable 'visibility' of the manufacturer's performance across the contract fulfilment process. This performance is captured in a range of measures. At the highest level will be the customer facing measures (e.g. lost passenger hours), then macro internal measures (e.g. train availability, reliability and performance), through to localized measures and indicators (e.g. performance against standard times for completing a task) (see section 6.1).

Overall, internal performance will be captured using management ratios for effectiveness and efficiency. These processes are people-centric, in that they rely to a large extent on people for their execution rather that automated systems. These people are engaged in a wide variety of roles. These might be in the frontline and interacting with the customer frequently (e.g. field engineers, account managers), or they may be supporting these roles (e.g. condition monitoring, parts and services managers) (see section 10.1).

The skill-sets of these people are highly influential upon or critical to the smooth operation of these processes (Table 10.2). Overall their behaviours can be described as humanistic; these people are skilled in being flexible, relationship builders, service-centric, authentic, technically adept and resilient. These skill-sets mean that they are well equipped to fulfil customers' expectations, even when unexpected events occur.

Among these, relationship building is a particularly valuable skill. We mentioned earlier how the relationship features of advanced services contracts are often seen to be distinctive. These relationships exist between people. They are more likely to be strong and healthy if staff are skilled in fostering such relationships.

Information and communication technologies feed into the contract fulfilment process. Much of this takes place in and around the control centre environment. In Figure 9.1 we showed the architecture of such systems. Processes link directly to this, helping to ensure that any necessary actions are instigated and followed through, informing and advancing actions on maintenance, repair and use.

The contract fulfilment processes affect decisions about organizational structure and supply chain integration – in the cases of manufacturers that are delivering advanced services successfully, design and production capabilities are retained where they are key to responsiveness and improvement (see section 8.2). For instance, where subassemblies are critical to the performance of the product but supply base capabilities are insufficient to rapidly respond should the subsystem fail in service, then the manufacturer will bring in-house the necessary production facilities.

A similar situation arises with facilities. Where these are co-located and distributed throughout customers' operations, then people are on-hand should there be an urgent need to respond (see section 7.1) – again, helping to ensure that the process is fulfilled.

11.4 Chapter Summary

A picture of a servitized manufacturer is emerging that is distinctly different to production. We see an organization that is integrated with its customers' operations, couple this with selected design and production capabilities, and has distributed facilities throughout the customers' operations, relying on sentient assets to trigger processes to deal proactively with issues, so that disruption to customers' operations is minimized. *But, how is this whole system being controlled?*

Business processes with advanced services are proactive and customer integrated. Policies are formed upfront around the desired outcomes from equipment usage. Should an impending failure become apparent, then the manufacturer must be prepared to respond within a tight time window, with corresponding rewards and penalties. Every effort must be made to minimize the impact of disruptions on the customers' operations, and close communication and cooperation are required.

Part 4
Readiness to Servitize

This final part draws a conclusion to this book and a bridge to the future. So far we have focused entirely on communicating the concepts of servitization and the practices and technologies that support the delivery of advanced services. This is one part of a story. Organizations also need to know how to servitize, where they should start, and the path they should follow to be most successful.

This change management raises a whole raft of new research questions, and far too many to do justice to in this final section alone. It is possible though to summarize the conditions that favour the take-up of servitization, within both sectors and individual businesses, and the factors that mainly determine whether adoption is likely to be a success. This therefore is the purpose of our final chapter.

In summary, in this part we:

Summarize servitization and advanced services, namely:

- Servitization is the process of transforming manufacturers to compete through services integrated with their products; a transition from production-centric to services-centric manufacture.

- Advanced services are a special case in servitization where the value proposition is based on the 'capabilities' that arise from the 'use' of the manufacturer's products.

- Advanced services are commonly combined with additional features (e.g. relationships over extended life-cycle, increased responsibilities (risks) for the manufacturer, and regular revenue payments).

- Delivery of advanced services demands a closely coupled system of practices and technologies.

Explore factors that indicate readiness for servitization, namely:

- Factors affecting the readiness of a business sector.

- Factors affecting the readiness of an individual manufacturer and its customers.

Convey that a transition to servitization is enabled by:

- Strong leadership.

- Informed and engaged customers.

- Platform for advanced services.

- People with humanistic skill-sets.

- Willingness to exploit technology.

- Willingness to form relationship-based strategic supply partnerships.

Chapter 12

In the 1980s and early 1990s many manufacturers looked at the concepts of Lean production with some scepticism. Today it's hard to imagine that companies would behave in the same way. Yet it has taken more than 30 years for these ideas to spread across industry.

Earlier we drew parallels between servitization and the early stages of Lean adoption. *So, can servitization spread faster?* Clearly we think that it's in every manufacturer's interests to adopt some aspects of servitization. Our motives are simple; servitization helps manufacturers to diversify and improve their commercial resilience, while environmentally it localizes activities and dematerializes the supply chain. Although these arguments are compelling, innovations take time to gain traction.

Early adopters are well known. Rolls-Royce earning around 50% of their revenue from services, for at least the past decade, is cited almost to exhaustion. *But which businesses are well positioned to follow?* Although business conditions increasingly favour servitization (Part 1), some industrial sectors and organizations are better placed than others. The challenge is to identify these.

In this chapter we examine conditions that favour servitization. This examination is at the levels of both business sector and individual organization. As a starting point, we begin by summarizing the principal features of servitization and advanced services, and how this world differs from that of production-centric manufacture. We close this chapter by identifying those aspects of the servitization journey where further study would aid widespread adoption within industry.

12.1 Summarizing Servitization, Advanced Services and their Delivery System

The general public understands the concept of a factory. Perceptions might be dated and lack precision, but most people can conjure an image of people working on production lines, carrying out machining and assembly tasks, to produce products that are then sold to customers. Such visualization is not so easy for servitization.

Our goal in this book has been to illuminate servitization and associated concepts. In Part 2 we explained servitization as a move to competing through advanced services, and in Part 3 we described the practices and technologies that constitute an effective delivery system for these. Our servitization roadmap (Figure 12.1) captures the princi-

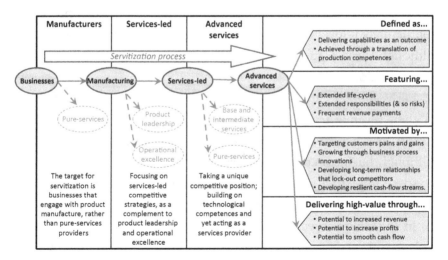

Figure 12.1: *A servitization roadmap*

pal features of servitization, and emphasizes that our particular focus is on those advanced services that can be of particularly high value to manufacturers.

Advanced services are a special case in servitization. These provide the customer with the 'capabilities' that arise from the 'use' of the manufacturer's products, and demand that the manufacturer extends itself significantly beyond its design and production-based competences. In many instances the manufacturer is moving into the territory of activities previously carried out by the customer, and in doing so is delivering capabilities that are a major component of the customer's core business processes.

Advanced services are commonly combined with additional features. Contract life-cycles tend to be long (5–15 years are common); the manufacturer takes on responsibility (and so risks) for ensuring that the capability performs as expected; and revenue payments are often coupled to usage. So prominent are these features that advanced services are frequently referred to in these terms. Performance contracting, availability contracts and risk and revenue sharing contracts are all terms that are commonly used to described advanced services.

Advanced services do not necessarily represent new business models, however, but simply business models that are new to many manufacturers. Often the services in question are already being performed by either the customers themselves or their service partners. The innovation here is that it is the manufacturer that is moving into this space. The motivations and benefits are striking. Frequently, the manufacturer's value to customers increases and intimate long-term relationships are created that lock out competitors. Ultimately this can lead to increased and more sustainable revenue generation and profits.

Successful servitization depends on a raft of factors. The manufacturer has to have the right product–service offering, for the right customer, for the right application, at the right time. While we explore some of these broader factors shortly, the bulk of our attention has focused on the organizational changes to the manufacturer.

Advanced services are delivered by product–service systems (PSS). The concept of a PSS frequently extends to incorporate financial mechanisms and the 'service delivery system'. This system demands that the operations of the manufacturer are configured radically differently to those of production. Facilities are co-located and distributed throughout customers' operations, integrated both forwards and backwards in their supply chains, and staffed by personnel who are flexible, relationship-building, service-centric, authentic, technically adept and resilient. These people work within business processes that are integrated into their customers' operations, and supported by ICT capabilities that enable remote product monitoring. The entire system is controlled by measures that reflect outcomes aligned to individual customers, and then cascade down into various forms throughout the service delivery system. These are implemented by tactics that demonstrate value broadly across operations.

This system is foundational to successful service delivery. These practices and technologies interconnect, interact, balance and compensate for each other as a system. When deployed, the nature and extent of their adoption will reflect the organizational context and the characteristics of the advanced services being offered. Yet they must come together and work as a system, fundamentally providing the manufacturer with:

- An ability to respond cost effectively.

- An ability to improve cost effectiveness.

The extent of the transformation should not be underestimated. For simplicity, servitization is often described as adding and integrating more and more services to products. This misrepresents the organizational transformation faced by a conventional manufacturer. Ultimately, servitization means shifting the manufacturer's operations from a production-centric to a services-centric paradigm. The manufacturer extends their operations beyond production, to deploy their products through advanced services. Table 12.1 illustrates differences between these two systems.

As a final note, there are many aspects of servitization and advanced services that initially appear confusing. Misunderstanding frequently occurs around:

- *Asset ownership:* Manufacturers still 'sell' their products, but ownership is typically transferred to a financial partner rather than the user. The customer then pays a regular monthly rate to cover financing and support service from the manufacturer.

- *Product–service system and service delivery system:* Product–service system refers to the total system that delivers the offering to the customer (including financial and supply partnerships), with the service delivery system being the subsystem that constitutes the operations of the manufacturer.

- *Manufacturing capabilities:* Servitization exploits manufacturing competences. It is *not* about becoming 'just' another services company. The technologies and practices needed to support the service delivery system are every bit as sophisticated as those in production.

- *Servitization and advanced services:* Advanced services are a particular form of service offering that characterizes servitization. Simply adding services to product platforms is also a form of servitization, but generally offers lower business potential.

12.2 A Readiness to Servitize

We did not set out to explore 'when to servitize', but our study naturally improved our understanding of when servitization is likely to

Table 12.1 Summarizing characteristics illustrating delivery system for advanced services

		Production-centric	Services-centric
Scope/focus		Design and production of products, which are then sold to customers	Design and production of products, which are then deployed as advanced services
Offering	*Form*	Product (or base services)	Advanced services
	Outcome	Product provision/ownership	Capability delivered through performance of the product
	Typically feature	Transactional sale / Warranty against failure / Lump revenue payment	Relationships over extended life-cycles / Extensive responsibilities, risks and penalties / Regular revenue payments
Delivery system characteristics	*Performance measures*	Focus on cost, quality and delivery of products	Focus on outcomes aligned to individual customers, which are then cascaded in various forms throughout the service delivery system, and complemented by indicators that broadly demonstrate value
	Facilities and their location	Centralized to exploit economies of scale, natural resources and access to markets	Develop or adopt facilities, co-located and distributed throughout customer's operations
	Vertical integration	Integrated where needed to control cost and quality	Extend beyond production, integrating into a wide range of customer activities, through extensive front-office activities aligned around services offered, with design and production capabilities in place to support through-life deployment
	ICT	Focus on the planning and control of material flow	Extend to inform and advancing actions on maintenance, repair and use
	People deployment and skills	Staff who are technically skilled, analytical and dependable	'Front-office' staff assigned who are skilled in being flexible, relationship builders, service-centric, authentic, technically adept and resilient
	Business processes	Reactive to demands for after-sales support and tendency towards 'heroic recovery'	Extend processes across a wide range of customer 'touch-points', fostering strong inter-organizational relationships at these, to manage proactively the condition, use and location of products in the field

gain traction. Factors became apparent for business sectors and individual manufacturers as to their readiness to compete through advanced services.

Factors indicating readiness of a business sector

Organizations adopt strategies that reflect their business environment. In Chapter 2 we looked at the market pull for services from an economic, environmental and market perspective. We also illustrated how manufacturers are increasingly enabled to exploit these opportunities through improvements in technology and the knowledge base. We concluded that a growth in the adoption of servitization is inevitable among western manufacturers.

Yet there are those industries that thrive on product ownership, especially for prestigious luxury items such as jewellery and expensive cars, where adoption will inevitably be slow. Indeed, in some industries the opportunity for services can appear to be eroding. Although it might make good sense environmentally to have collective services such as launderettes, stronger market and social factors drive product ownership.

Servitization is therefore most likely in a business sector where certain conditions are fulfilled. Our analysis in Chapter 2 indicates these conditions and Table 12.2 has been formed around these main points. Each has been rephrased as a question. The greater the number of these questions that can be answered 'yes', the more likely that servitization could be a valuable response and so gain traction in the sector. This process is intended to be insightful rather than a mechanistic analysis. Three examples from western Europe help to illustrate this point namely the machine tool, automotive and clothing sectors.

Machine tool manufacturers in Europe are exposed to severe economic pressures. Their products are relatively easy to transport and

Table 12.2 Factors indicating the readiness of a business sector for servitization

	Questions for the industrial sector
Economic	• Are the main markets for your products in Europe and North America? • Do these products have a long shelf-life? • Are they easily transported and imported? • Is brand independent of where products are produced? • Do products have a high labour content? • Are they produced in volume? • Are there only few opportunities for new product innovation? • Are there only few opportunities for radical cost reduction? • Are innovations difficult to defend? • Is the installed base of products (those already in the field) significant? • Might there be opportunities to grow revenue through services to this installed base?
Environmental	• Does production consume high levels of energy and/or materials? • Does product operation consume high levels of energy and/or materials? • Could this energy and material be reduced by offering services rather than products? • Might credentials as a 'green' organization aid competitiveness?
Markets/social	• Would services offerings be easy to defend from product substitution? • Might the appetite for services themselves be increasing? • Could products open new opportunities for services? • Are there opportunities to offer services that incorporate products?
Technologies	• Are services more appealing when there is 'visibility' of product? • Might ICT capabilities help to provide such visibility? • Are ICT capabilities readily available and accessible?

Table 12.2 (*Continued*)

	Questions for the industrial sector
Knowledge	• *Would business be open to the following ideas:* • *That customers only gain value from your product as they use it?* • *That the operations needed to effectively support services differ from production?* • *That organizational structures, principles and processes might need to change?* • *That services might offer a long-term sustainable business model?* • *That services are delivered by a system of products, people, technology and business?*

expensive to manufacture, product innovation demands significant expertise and investment, and opportunities for cost reduction are low. Yet the installed base is high and brings with it opportunities for services. Environmental factors also favour services. Given the right incentives the machine tool manufacturers have significant opportunity to reduce the energy consumed by their equipment and consumables such as cutting fluids. Machine tool technologies are readily informated, and so remote monitoring is relatively easy. Perhaps the most significant barriers to servitization are around the awareness and engagement among customers and manufacturers. Even then, there is a growing number of applications now being reported in the machine tool sector.

In the automotive sector businesses are larger, volumes greater and services more developed. Yet the environmental pressures are more acute and the service offerings and infrastructure more advanced. One of the leading examples currently is Peugeot leasing. Their sales pitch is 'just add fuel'. Peugeot takes care of all servicing, car tax, warranty, breakdown cover and comprehensive insurance, which are paid for by regular monthly instalments over three years. However, many of these leasing models are yet to capture the essence of advanced services (they operate at the level of car availability rather than the customer's 'need for mobility').

This is poised to change. As the world's economies move out of recession, environmental pressures will undoubtedly intensify. Fuel consumption, emissions and recycling will come under increasing scrutiny. Consequently, we are already seeing the advent of niche producers who are developing services offerings where they provide the fuel for the car. Couple this to stringent agreements for car availability, penalties if this is not provided, and pay-as-you-go revenue streams, and automotive manufacturers are well on their way to offering advanced service.

Fashion and clothing differ considerably from the first two examples. They are often dismissed prematurely; volumes are high, materials and technologies are simple and established, consumerism is rife, and cost of ownership low. Yet some surprising innovations are taking place. Some companies have recognized that for high-value designer clothing some customers value a rental service; the experience they seek is to wear or be seen in a particular outfit on a special occasion. The customer can select their outfit over the web, have it sent by post to their home and return it the same way.

This is an embryonic example and it is pure-service providers (rather than producers) that are doing this (hence not true servitization). Yet, with a little imagination, it is possible to see how producers themselves can offer similar services – perhaps coupling these services to rapid design and production facilities, located close to their customers, and RFID (Radio Frequency Identification) tags to monitor usage and condition. Clearly there is a very long way to go for such models to revolutionize the fashion and clothing industry, but they help to illustrate the broad opportunities that exist for servitization.

Factors indicating readiness of a manufacturing business

Time and time again during this study we have been asked to suggest the conditions under which servitization is appropriate (or not) to individual companies. All too often the conversation centres on the complexity of the product, the costs of ownership and risks to the customer if there is an in-service failure. Having studied a wide range of businesses, both big and small, we now appreciate that there are some more fundamental determinants around the suitability of servitization.

Quite simply the manufacturing company has to be healthy. Servitization is not a quick-fix for a poorly run operation, as more (rather than less) strain is placed on the business; it builds onto, rather than substitutes, leading thinking such as Lean principles and Six Sigma. Nor are excellent services a substitute for unreliable products; they demand that the products perform well if they are to be delivered cost effectively.

For those manufacturers capable of servitizing, there are subsequent factors that indicate the readiness for them to compete through advanced services. Ultimately the manufacturer has to be motivated to change from conventional production. Our leading adopters of servitization shared similar motives (see Chapter 4). Rephrased, these suggest a set of circumstances that can inspire a manufacturer and their customers to seriously consider offering advanced services (Table 12.3).

Motives simply reflect a willingness to consider servitization. Adoption depends on a further set of factors (Table 12.4). Key factors include the performance of products, understanding of application, detailed knowledge of costs and experience of financing arrangements. The longer good relationships have been in place, the greater this confidence becomes. Caterpillar illustrates this well. Many of their dealers have been in place for over 50 years, and they themselves

Table 12.3 Motives for servitization

Manufacturers can be motivated towards advanced services when:	Customers can be motivated towards advanced services when:
They see opportunities to help customers to be more successful by offering services that improve their business processes	They seek to reduce operating costs and risks but improve product/asset performance
They see opportunities to grow business revenue by opening up new streams with existing customers	They want their management team to focus energies on core business activities
They are striving to lock out competitors and establish long-term resilient cash-flow streams	They seek to transfer fixed costs into variable costs that reflect revenue generation, and also improve financial visibility

Table 12.4 Factors affecting the readiness of an individual company for servitization

Factor	Manufacturers are likely to offer advanced services when they have:	Customers are likely to adopt advanced services when they have:
Culture	A customer who will use the product correctly and within the terms of a contract	Culture (and willingness) to focus on their own core business activities
Relationships	Reliable and trustworthy relationship between themselves/their customers/ and their supply partners	Reliable and trustworthy relationships between the manufacturer/themselves/ and their own customers
Application	Customer's applications where there is repeatability in the location and the way the product is used	A manufacturer who can demonstrate that it understands the particular application
Product	A broad platform of reliable products well suited to the application	A manufacturer who can demonstrate a broad platform of reliable products well suited to the application

Table 12.4 (*Continued*)

Factor	Manufacturers are likely to offer advanced services when they have:	Customers are likely to adopt advanced services when they have:
Costs	Thorough understanding of current costs incurred by the customer and likely future costs for themselves	Thorough understanding of current and likely future costs for themselves
Capitalization	Access to financial arrangements enabling product acquisition	A manufacturer who can offer financial arrangements to funding product acquisition
Contracts	Appropriate risk and revenue sharing contracts between themselves, their customers and their supply partners	A manufacturer who develops a reliable risk and revenue sharing contract
Visibility	Capability that provides visibility of the health, performance and usage of the product as it is operated	A manufacturer who can offer and share visibility of the performance and usage of the product as it is operated
Support	Confidence that their organizational capabilities for service delivery are effective and efficient	Confidence that the manufacturer has the organizational capabilities to deliver the contract

have similar lengthy relationships with many customers. This is a tremendous legacy that underpins their ability to deliver advanced services.

The factors in Tables 12.3 and 12.4 indicate when servitization is likely to gain traction within an organization. Ultimately companies have individual choices to make as to the benefits of pursuing a servitization strategy. Even when the intention is strong, there are obstacles that can get in the way of a successful transition.

12.3 Overcoming the Obstacles to Transformation

Visualizing servitization and the factors affecting readiness is only half of the challenge. Even when the opportunity gains traction practitioners commonly ask: *how can we servitize successfully, how should we go about the transformation process, where do we start?*

More work is needed before we can answer these questions with conviction. Yet, in conducting our research, we naturally experienced a wide range of practitioners describing the obstacles they had faced in their servitization journey. More helpfully they gave us insights into how they had navigated these successfully.

The starting position is fundamental. For a well-run manufacturer rooted in products and production, the challenges of organizational transformation are considerable. These proliferate if the business itself has elementary problems. As we have highlighted, servitization is not an 'instead of' or 'easy option' for companies that are struggling to succeed. Delivering advanced services is every bit as demanding as production, and the consequences of failing to perform can be more severe.

The transformation strategy therefore has to be well formulated and deployed. Change management challenges are inevitable, some of which are heightened by the idiosyncrasy of the topic. During our study the following factors were frequently cited as enablers:

- *Strong leadership:* Having in place senior executives who have a clear understanding of servitization and its nuances, can articulate these well, and have the conviction and interpersonal skills to see this through to execution.

- *Informed and engaged customers:* Having customers who are willing to engage and co-deliver service offerings. Recognizing that larger corporations are often more bold, wanting to proactively focus on their core competences, while smaller family owned businesses can appear reluctant and more comfortable with product design, production and sales.

- *Platform for advanced services:* Already having in place an effective 'front office' dealing with base and intermediate services, along with strong internal relationships that foster support from the wider manufacturing organization.

- *People with humanistic skill-set:* Already having in place key people with a service skill-set. Recognizing that such people are very different to those in production, and that alternative recruitment and incentive schemes are often necessary.

- *Willingness to exploit technology:* Having an awareness of ICT capabilities and the skills to exploit these. Yet recognizing that many aspects of such capabilities are now readily accessible to all organizations, and as such unlikely to provide sustained competitive advantage.

- *Willingness to form relationship-based strategic supply partnerships:* Having a willingness to form risk and reward sharing partnerships with those suppliers who can support the delivery of an advanced service. Yet recognizing that vertical integration into design and production competences is often necessary where suppliers can't provide the necessary responsiveness and business improvements.

Expectations are also high. There is a familiar innovation cycle; initially expectations are inflated, disillusionment follows, then enlightenment, and finally acknowledgement. This is not, however, virgin territory. Some manufacturers are already relatively mature in their adoption of servitization, others are seeking innovation in their service offerings, while others still are innovating their delivery systems to completely revitalize long forgotten services. A danger is to look at servitization only from the viewpoint of new and alternative service offerings, and to ignore the potential of a closely coupled service delivery system. There are undoubtedly routes to follow which are likely to deliver more successes than others. Understanding these is a significant challenge, and naturally leads to discussing future directions for research.

12.4 The Journey Continues

Servitization is a concept and the concept is not new; examples exist from the 1800s. What is new is our consolidation and formalization of knowledge about servitization so that the opportunities can be widely accessed.

Servitization goes to the core of how the manufacturer sees itself vis-à-vis its customers. Rather than seeing itself as providing value mainly through the design and sale of goods or technologies, it becomes a provider of functional capabilities that are delivered by the physical assets that it produces. Such a change in strategy has big implications for the way that the manufacturing firm is organized, how decisions are made and the influence that the service providing arm of the firm has in setting strategies, designing products and assigning resources.

Those immersed in the delivery of advanced services see the world differently to those in production; it is difficult to treat this as anything other than a paradigm shift. For those seeking to compete through advanced services, practices cannot be adopted in isolation; an integrated product–service delivery system has to be created to complement the offering made to the customer. The situation is reminiscent of Just-in-Time adoption in the late 1980s, where companies sought to adopt Kanban without reducing setup times, simplifying flow, developing suppliers and balancing schedules.

The picture of successful servitization is still evolving for manufacturing companies, and so too is our understanding of this strategy. Opportunities for growth and competitive advantage appear to be present in many industries, especially as profit potentials from manufacturing-only business models continue to decline in the industrialized world.

On concluding this study we feel that manufacturers have just begun to value servitization. *What is holding them back, and where are innovations needed?* In our view, the most fundamental barrier is the language and mindsets held by many in both the academic and industrial communities. Manufacturers are seen as different to service providers; products different to services. As we examined earlier (section 3.1), production people often struggle to appreciate the value of services, and services people frequently fail to grasp the potential of engineering and production competences. Overcoming the prejudice is perhaps our biggest challenge.

Finally, we have not set out in this book to blindly advocate servitization and advanced services, but rather to explain them in such a way that they become accessible to a wider range of manufacturers. It is, though, essential to take a particular view about servitization. Some people treat servitization as a manufacturer increasing their volume of business in what we have described as base and intermediate services. Others celebrate how organizations such as IBM have created a new future for themselves by moving away from their traditional manufacturing-based businesses and into services-based originations. Both these views are valuable and hold potential for organizations.

Our concern is, however, different. In this book we have treated servitization as a manufacturer increasing their focus on what we term as advanced services. A move from services supporting 'the product' to services supporting 'the customer'. Undoubtedly some will see these as simply a special case in servitization. Yet we strongly advocate these for their high-value potential to impact the wealth and resilience of manufacturing, and to fundamentally improve environmental and social sustainability.

Appendix

The genesis of this book lies with studies carried out in the late 1990s exploring the concept of 'Total Service Manufacture'. These were published by, among others, the Department of Trade and Industry in the UK. They reflected a growing recognition that as the adoption of Lean techniques by industry matured, and the associated benefits became widespread, then alternative means of competitive differentiation would be sought by manufacturers. These coincided with our own experiences of practising, researching and consulting for industry, and stimulated our interest in manufacturers competing through services.

In 2006 we gained the support of the Engineering and Physical Sciences Research Council in the UK to investigate servitization and PSS. We joined collaborations and friendships with likeminded researchers that have endured ever since. We remain especially grateful to David Stephenson, Andy Neely, Joe Peppard, Steve Evans, Raj Roy, Rick Greenough, Veronica Martinez, Mark Johnson, Essam Shehab, Ashutosh Tiwari, David Tranfield, Palie Smart and John Kay. We also gained inspiration from some exceptional researchers and their publications. These included:

- Chase, R. and Garvin, D. (1989) The Service Factory, *Harvard Business Review*, **67**(4), 61–69.

- Gebauer, H., Fischer, T. and Fleisch, E. (2004) Overcoming the Service Paradox in Manufacturing Companies, *European Management Journal*, **23**(1), 14–26.

- Mont, O. (2000) Product–Service Systems, *Final Report for IIIEE*, Lund University.

- Oliva, R. and Kallenberg, R. (2003) Managing the Transition from Products to Services, *International Journal of Service Industry Management*, **14**(2), 1–10.

- Spohrer, J., Maglio, P., Bailey, J. and Gruhl, D. (2007) Steps Towards a Science of Service Systems, *Computer*, January, 71–77.

- Tukker, A. (2004) Eight Types of Product Service System; Eight Ways to Sustainability? Experiences from SUSPRONET, *Business Strategy and the Environment*, **13**, 246–260.

- Vargo, S. and Lusch, R. (2004) Evolving to a new dominant logic for marketing, *Journal of Marketing*, **68**, 1–71

- Voss, C. (1992) Applying Service Concepts in Manufacturing, *International Journal of Operations and Production Management*, **12**(4), 93–99.

- Vandermerwe, S. and Rada, J. (1988) Servitization of Business: Adding Value by Adding Services, *European Management Journal*, **6**(4).

- Wise, R. and Baumgartner, P. (1999) Go Downstream: The New Profit Imperative in Manufacturing, *Harvard Business Review*, Sept./Oct., 133–141.

At this time the concepts of servitization and PSS were not widely understood, rarely integrated, and frequently lacking in their recognition of achievements by industry. We consequently sought to consolidate our knowledge. We were particularly fortunate to be able to study Rolls-Royce Plc to gain a preliminary understanding of their advanced services offerings and how they were delivered. For this, we are especially grateful for the support of Miles Cowdry, Jonathan Throssell, Ian Callendar, Neil Brown, Peter Roberts, Ian Jennions, Tim Plant, Rob Hill, Malcolm Watling, Mark Reddish, Jane MacDonald and other colleagues at Rolls-Royce. Indeed, we have remained in contact with Rolls-Royce throughout this programme and would also like to acknowledge the subsequent help and support of Andy Harrison and Charlie Dibsdale.

In complement, we also reviewed and consolidated the research literature, widely surveyed industrial practice, and set out our initial ideas of how organizations would be configured when fully servitized. Among the many people who helped us through this process, we are especially grateful to Dan Whitney (Massachusetts Institute of Technology), Morgan Swink (Texas Christian University) and Ornella Benedettini (Politecnico di Bari, Italy). This knowledge was captured in a variety of publications, including:

- Baines, T., Lightfoot, H., Evans, S., Neely, A., Greenough, R., Peppard, J., Roy, R., Shehab, E., Braganza, A., Tiwari, A., Alcock, J., Angus, J., Bastl, M., Cousens, A., Irving, P., Johnson, M., Kingston, J., Lockett, H., Martinez. V., Micheli, P., Tranfield, D., Walton, I. and Wilson, H. (2007) State-of-the-Art in Product Service-Systems, *Proc. IMechE Part B: Journal of Engineering Manufacture*, **221**, 1543–1533.

- Baines, T.S., Lightfoot, H., Benedettini, O., Whitney, D. and Kay, J.M. (2010) The Adoption of Servitization Strategies by UK based Manufacturers, *IJMechE Part B*, **224**(5), 815–830.

- Baines, T.S., Lightfoot, H. and Benedettini, O. (2009) The Servitization of Manufacturing: A Review of the Literature, *Journal of Technology Management*, **20**(5), 547–567.

- Baines, T.S., Lightfoot, H. and Kay, J.M. (2009) Servitized Manufacture: Practical Challenges of Delivering Integrated Products and Services, *IJMechE Part B*, **223**(1–9), 1207–1215.

- Baines, T.S., Lightfoot, H., Peppard, J., Johnson, M., Tiwari, A., Shehab, E. and Swink, M. (2009) Towards an Operations Strategy for Product-centric Servitization, *International Journal of Operations and Production Management*, **29**(5), 494–519.

Our understanding progressed from this foundation. Central to this was our in-depth study of Caterpillar and selected dealerships, MAN Truck and Bus UK, Xerox and Alstom Transport. We were fortunate to gain outstanding support from a broad range of employees from each of these organizations, and would particularly like to recognize the help and guidance of:

- Caterpillar Inc., Peoria, USA: Jon Greiner and Heng Zhou, along with Bob Wille, Andy Wendling and Anthony Mountjoy.

- Caterpillar dealerships: Dave Barta and Mike Glen (Wagner Equipment, Colorado); Jim Kenagy and Ben Romney (Wheeler Machinery, Utah); Mike Johnson and Richard Black (Hawthorne Machinery); Mike Hulon, Dyke Rasco and Justin Homann (Mustang Machinery, Texas); Bob Bacon and Terrill Surrett (Thompson Tractor, Alabama); Joe Swayne and Tim Huffman (Yancy Bros, Georgia); and Paul Ryder and Marcus Pitt (Finning, UK).

- MAN Truck and Bus, UK: Des Evans, Dennis Evans, David Cussons, Derek Mensing, Andy Turner, David Lester, John Davis, Vince Welsh and Geoff du Plessis.

- Xerox, UK: Andy Jones, Zac Emmett, Jonathan Leaper, Nigel Smith, Chris Pickering, Paul Gaiser and Alicia Cuadra.

- Alstom Transport UK: Mike Hulme, Alex Stephenson, Martin Higson, Pierre Baupre, Tom Fallon, Andy Grabham, Justin Southcombe, Roy Sullivan, Tim Bentley, Adrian Grigg, Piers Wood, Michel Marien and Jean-Francois Blanc.

We broadened our understanding of technologies and practices by carrying out nine supplementary cases and would like to acknowledge the help and support of Ian Colville (Aculab), Jason Abbott (Knorr-Bremse), Mark Smith (Weatherite), Sally White (Smiths Detection), Terry Newby (SSP Pumps), Richard Guest (Froude Hofmann), Reg Gott (Nuaire), Kevin Wright (Baker Perkins), Brett Sanders (Snell) and Chris Allen (Meggitt Aircraft Braking).

Simultaneously our academic network matured, and a range of researchers both at home and abroad gave us help and support in various ways. We are especially grateful to Tim McAloone (Technical University, Denmark), Horst Meier (Bochum University, Germany), Gunter Zieliger (TU Berlin, Germany), Jan Holstrom and Saara Brax (Helsinki University of Technology, Finland), Arnold Tukker (TNO, Delft, Holland), Carlo Vezzoli (Politecnico University Milan, Italy), Heiko Gebauer, EWAG, Switzerland and Jay Lee (University of Cincinnati, USA). Also from the UK Martin Spring (Lancaster University), Irene Ng (Exeter University), Chris Voss (LBS), Andy Davis (Imperial College), Duncan McFarlane (Cambridge University), Alison McKay (Leeds University) and Ken Green (Manchester University).

We also found a number of articles particularly helpful at this time, and these included:

- Brax, S. (2005) A Manufacturer Becoming Service Provider – Challenges and a Paradox. *Manufacturing Service Quality*, **15**(2), 142–156.

- Davies, A., Brady, T. and Hobday, M. (2006) Charting a Path Towards Integrated Solutions, *MIT Sloan Management Review*, **43**(7), 39–48.

- Gronroos, C. (2008) Service Logic Revisited: Who Creates Value? And Who Co-creates, *European Business Review*, **20**(4), 298–314.

- Mathieu, V. (2001) Service Strategies within the Manufacturing Sector: Benefits, Costs and Partnership, *International Journal of Service Industry Management*, **12**(5), 451–475.

- Machuca, J. and Gonzalez-Zamora, M. (2007) Service Operations Management Research, *JOM*, **25**, 585–603.

- Neely, A. (2009) Exploring the Financial Consequences of the Servitization of Manufacturing, *Operations Management Research*, **1**(2).

- Spring, M. and Araujo, L. (2009) Service and Products: Rethinking Operations Strategy, *Journal of Operations and Production Management*, **29**(5), 444–467.

We consolidated and communicated our findings through a range of research publications. In particular:

- Organising for Services Growth and Productivity within Manufacturing, Report to the Royal Academy of Engineering, *INGENIA*, **44**, 36–39, Sept. 2010.

- Lightfoot, H., Baines, T. and Smart, P. (2011) Examining the Information and Communication Technologies Enabling Servitized Manufacture, *IJMechE Part B*, **225**(10), 1964–1968.

- Baines, T., Lightfoot, H. and Smart, P. (2011) Servitization within Manufacturing Operations: An Exploration of the Impact to Facilities Practices, *IJMechE Part B*, **226**(2), 377–380.

- Baines, T., Lightfoot, H. and Smart, P. (2011) Servitization within Manufacturing: Exploring the Provision of Advanced Services and their Impact on Vertical Integration, *Journal of Technology Management*, **22**(7), 947–954.

- *Financial Times* (2012) UK Groups Lag Behind in Adding Services, http://www.ft.com/intl/cms/s/0/890ae896-a1bd-11e1-ae4c-00144feabdc0.html#axzz1wKrwCKVX. 30 May.

On the conclusion of our investigations and compilation of this book several practitioners have kindly reviewed the text and made suggestions on how it can be improved. We are immensely grateful to Jon Greiner, Bob Bacon, Mike Hulon, Bob Wille, Paul Ryder, Martin Higson, Mike Hulme, Tim Bentley, Tom Fallon, Andy Jones, Zac Emmett, Des Evans and Andy Harrison for their feedback and encouragement in delivering this text.

INDEX

Index compiled by Indexing Specialists (UK) Ltd

Printed in the United States
By Bookmasters